Vocabulary in Context

an intensive course in English
English Language Institute

Vocabulary in Context
Harry B. Franklin
Herbert G. Meikle
and Jeris E. Strain

Ann Arbor   The University of Michigan Press

ISBN 0-472-08305-8
Published in the United States of America by
The University of Michigan Press
Manufactured in the United States of America

1994   1993   1992   1991   25   24   23   22

Preface

THIS BOOK follows basically the same linguistic and pedagogical principles that were followed in earlier editions of the *Lessons in Vocabulary* of the Intensive Course in English. Thus, it embodies much of the methodology of Charles C. Fries, Robert Lado, and their many co-workers, who produced the original Institute textbooks. The application of the structural approach to the design of oral drills in vocabulary was mainly the work of Edward M. Anthony.

As a result of the revision that has been going on without interruption since 1956, the present volume must be considered an entirely new work. All of the material has been thoroughly tested in the classroom. The chief aim has been to bring these lessons into closer coordination with the revised editions of the Grammar and Pattern Practice books, which are published separately as part of the Intensive Course in English.

The Introduction for the Teacher summarizes the principles on which the lessons are based and provides specific suggestions for their use.

The chief responsibility for the preparation of this volume was assumed by the three named authors, with the help of Edward M. Palumbo and Donald L. F. Nilsen. The statistical analysis of the vocabulary of the entire intensive course was done by Andreas Koutsoudas and Riza E. Ellis. To give credit for every contribution and suggestion incorporated in the book would be to list the entire staff of the English Language Institute.

HAROLD V. KING

Teacher's Introduction

This text is one part of "An Intensive Course in English." The other three parts emphasize the mastery of English sounds *(Pronunciation)*, grammatical structures *(Sentence Patterns)*, and the formation of automatic habits *(Pattern Practices)*. This one emphasizes the development of skill in using those sounds, structures, and habits in everyday situations. It should, therefore, be used in conjunction with the other three.

One of the principles of "An Intensive Course in English" is that the teacher should begin with a structural point and work toward situations in which it occurs. This structural approach has two advantages. First, the lessons can deal primarily with such things as tense, verb categories, noun categories, and groups of function words. Second, the lessons can follow a systematic development of the essential grammatical framework.

In this text one of the main roles of vocabulary is to provide a few situations in which the structural points learned in other parts of the course occur. Another is to anticipate the items that will be needed in teaching grammatical structures. The third is to review and expand the use of items and structures already taught, adding additional lexical material within this framework.

The primary device for presenting vocabulary material in these lessons is the dialogue. It not only provides flexibility in combining structures and lexical items to form situations but also is a very effective device for stimulating conversation.

The procedure regularly followed in presenting new material is as follows: *attention pointer, presentation, generalization, practice*.

The *attention pointer* is used to call attention to the lexical area or items that are taught.

The *presentation* is a conversation in which the items being taught are illustrated and defined by context. A "Situation" often provides the setting. The structures in the corresponding grammar lesson generally form the underlying framework of the conversation; structures taught previously may also be included. As for lexical items, in addition to those being taught, there may also be items taught previously, items being anticipated, items closely related to another item, and conventional phrases.

A *generalization* is included as a "Note" when it seems necessary to bring out a specific point about the lexical items being taught. When the items are either defined in the presentation or are groups of words related to a special topic, such as foods, professions, or sizes, the generalization is omitted.

The *practice* is usually a drill exercise. It is aimed at increasing the student's fluency in using both the grammatical structures being reinforced and the lexical items being taught. For the most part, the practice is a conversation between the teacher and a student, the teacher asking questions that apply to the student's own situation. When a special problem is taught, one based on contrastive analysis (make-do, try-intend, know-meet), it is usually followed by a test exercise, one in which the two items are contrasted in various contexts.

Each lesson consists of three or more different teaching points. In addition, the first nine lessons contain review and summary dialogues; the student should be encouraged to memorize these. Beginning with Lesson XI, review questions replace the dialogues. Lessons X, XX, and XXX are review lessons.

The first lessons treat general cultural areas; the last lessons treat such large technical areas as the university, geography, government, and politics. The focus shifts from simple conversations in the first lessons to comprehension passages in the last lessons. Several word-building affixes are taught and two-word verbs are given special emphasis, particularly in the last ten lessons.

Written homework is suggested at the end of the first ten lessons to encourage the student to think in English and develop his command of the material and situations covered. The review questions provided in the remaining lessons may also be written out by the student or gone over in class. The last ten lessons provide topics which can be used as a basis for elementary compositions.

There are a few guidelines that the teacher might keep in mind. First of all, only a minimum of vocabulary items (and only the principal meanings of each) have been treated; the teacher is encouraged to expand this minimum to meet the requirements of his specific teaching situation. Second, the lessons are not word-centered nor definition-centered. They emphasize usage, that is, development of the student's ability to use vocabulary items in free and meaningful conversation. Third, the lessons are written for intermediate students who have had some contact with English, visual or otherwise, but who have had little opportunity to converse in it. Accordingly, classroom work should be entirely oral. Fourth, the style of English presented is polite colloquial, not formal and not slang.

Student's Introduction

1. These lessons are different from most vocabulary lessons. They do not teach words. They teach HOW TO USE words. They teach CONVER-SATION.

2. The lessons are not for a particular language background. They teach situations that every student must learn.

3. The lessons are for intermediate students. They are for students who have learned some English, but who have had little opportunity to use it.

4. Your other classes teach sentence patterns and pronunciation. This class teaches you to use those skills in specific situations—greeting friends, eating, shopping, asking directions, etc.

5. You may think, "I already know these words." BUT, can you use them? You have, of course, seen or read or heard some of the words taught in these lessons, but have you spoken them? Have YOU used them in con-versations? There are probably a few new expressions in each lesson that you do not know. There are probably a few more that you think are the same as words in your language; you will discover that they are quite different.

6. The lessons provide only a few expressions for each situation. You can help your teacher and yourself by studying the situations and asking ques-tions.

7. You should memorize the Summary Dialogues and the Review Dialogues. You should also learn the conversations; these have lines drawn around them.

8. When you learn the conversations and memorize the dialogues, always practice them with your classmates and your friends. Conversation re-quires at least TWO people.

Contents

Lesson I

A. HELLO, GOODBYE, EXCUSE ME, THANK YOU.
B. DOCTOR, CLERK, ENGINEER, etc.
C. BUSY, HUNGRY, NICE, TIRED, RIGHT, HAPPY, etc.

Dialogue. (Memorize.)

    John: Hello. My name is John.
    Juan: How do you do. My name is Juan.
    John: Are you Spanish?
    Juan: No, I'm not. I'm Mexican.

PERSON	COUNTRY	NATIONALITY
Pedro	Mexico	Mexican
Carlos	Colombia	Colombian
João	Brazil	Brazilian
Antonio	Italy	Italian
Mr. Zivari	Iran	Iranian
Ahmet	Turkey	Turkish (a Turk)
Jan	Poland	Polish (a Pole)
Lars	Sweden	Swedish (a Swede)
Mr. Lee	China	Chinese
Mr. Saito	Japan	Japanese
Nam	Vietnam	Vietnamese
Mr. Mwambai	Congo	Congolese
Pierre	France	French (a Frenchman)
Ernst	Germany	German
Demetrius	Greece	Greek
Manat	Thailand	Thai

NOTE: -AN (Mexican), -ISH (Turkish), -ESE (Japanese), etc.
         indicate nationality.

≡ A.1a   Observe Greetings.

In the morning (6 a.m. to 12 noon)	GOOD MORNING, Juan.
In the afternoon (12 noon to 6 p.m.)	GOOD AFTERNOON, Mr. Ito.
In the evening (6 p.m. to midnight)	GOOD EVENING, Miss Taylor.
General informal greeting	HELLO, John.
Very informal greeting	HI, Tony.

Exercise 1.1 Give the correct greetings. Use GOOD MORNING, GOOD AFTERNOON, and GOOD EVENING[1].

Examples: Teacher   Student

It's 10 a.m.   Student A. Good morning.
                      Student B. Good morning.

It's 4 p.m.   Student C. Good afternoon.
                      Student D. Good afternoon.

1. It's 8 p.m.	6. It's 2 p.m.	11. It's 10 a.m.
2. It's 11 a.m.	7. It's 8 p.m.	12. It's 8 p.m.
3. It's 2 p.m.	8. It's 8 a.m.	13. It's 6 a.m.
4. It's 7 a.m.	9. It's 1 p.m.	14. It's 5 p.m.
5. It's 7 p.m.	10. It's 8 p.m.	15. It's 9 p.m.

Ξ A.1b   Observe HOW ARE YOU.

John: Good morning. HOW ARE YOU?

Juan: Fine, thanks. HOW ARE YOU?

John: Very well, thank you.

NOTE: An informal answer is FINE THANKS, AND YOU?

Exercise 1.2   Use HOW ARE YOU with a greeting.

Example: Teacher   Student

It's 10 a.m.   Student A. Good morning. How ARE you?
                      Student B. Fine, thanks. How are YOU?
                      Student A. Very well, thank you.

1. It's 9 p.m.	4. It's 7 a.m.	7. It's 10 a.m.
2. It's 11 a.m.	5. It's 7 p.m.	8. It's 4 p.m.
3. It's 2 p.m.	6. It's 3 p.m.	9. It's 8 p.m.

Ξ A.1c   Observe Parting expressions.

General parting expression	GOOD-BYE, Juan[2].
Six p.m. to midnight	GOOD NIGHT, John.
Very informal expressions	SEE YOU LATER, Bill.
	SO LONG, Bob.

NOTES TO TEACHER: [1]Exercise 1.1 gives practice in the recognition of time expressions. "10 a.m.," etc.

[2]Emphasize that GOOD-BYE is only for leave-taking; some students use it erroneously when simply passing someone on the street.

Exercise 1.3   Give the correct expressions.

Examples: Teacher   Student

        It's 10 a.m. You arrive.   A. Good morning.
                                          B. Good morning.

        It's 5 p.m. You leave.   C. Good-bye.
                                          D. Good-bye.

  1. It's 10 a.m.   You arrive.
  2. It's 10 a.m.   You leave.
  3. It's 9 p.m.   You arrive.
  4. It's 10 p.m.   You leave.
  5. It's 10 p.m. or 10 a.m.   You arrive.
  6. It's 3 p.m.   You arrive.
  7. It's 8 a.m.   You arrive.
  8. It's 8 p.m.   You leave.
  9. It's 8 p.m. or 8 a.m.   You leave.
10. It's 2 p.m. or 11 p.m.   You leave.

≡ A.2   Observe expressions of Pardon.

John walks in front of Mr. Taylor.	John :	EXCUSE ME.
	Mr. Taylor:	CERTAINLY.
John, Mary, and Bill are eating. John leaves.	John :	EXCUSE ME PLEASE.
	Bill:	SURELY.
John interrupts a conversation.	John :	PARDON ME.
Mary is helping Mrs. Taylor. Mary spills coffee on the table.	Mary:	I'M SORRY.
	Mrs. Taylor:	THAT'S ALL RIGHT.

NOTE: I BEG YOUR PARDON is very formal.

Exercise 1.4 Practice EXCUSE ME, CERTAINLY, etc.

Example: Teacher   Student

        Mr. A and Mr. B are eat-   A. Excuse me, please.
          ing. Mr. A leaves.   B. Surely.

  1. Mr. C walks in front of Mr. D.
  2. Miss E is helping Mrs. F. Miss E spills milk on the table.
  3. Mr. G and Mr. H are eating. Mr. G leaves.
  4. Mrs. I interrupts the class.
  5. Miss J walks in front of Miss K.
  6. Mr. A interrupts the teacher.
  7. Mr. B is helping Miss C. Mr. B spills water on the table.

≡ A.3   Observe expressions of Gratitude.

Situation: John finds a pencil.

> John: Is this your pencil, Mary?
> Mary: Yes, it is. THANK YOU.
> John: YOU'RE WELCOME.
>
> -
>
> (John compliments Mary.)
>
> John: You look very nice today.
> Mary: THANK YOU.

Exercise 1.5   Practice THANK YOU and YOU'RE WELCOME.

Examples:	Teacher	Student
	Mr. A finds a book.	A. Is this your book?
		B. Yes, it is. Thank you.
		A. You're welcome.
	Mr. C compliments Miss D.	C. Your hair looks very nice.
		D. Thank you.

1. Mr. E finds a pen.
2. Mr. G finds a pencil.
3. Mr. I compliments Miss J.

4. Mr. A compliments Mrs. B.
5. Miss C finds a book.
6. Mr. E compliments Mr. F.

Exercise 1.6 Pronunciation exercise. (Please look at the pictures,
page 5. Repeat after the teacher.)

1. a doctor
   Mr. Green's a doctor.

2. a secretary
   Miss Green's a secretary.

3. a clerk
   John's a clerk.

4. a housewife
   Mrs. Taylor's a housewife.

5. an engineer
   Bill's an engineer.

6. a businessman
   Mr. Brown's a businessman.

7. an architect
   Mr. Smith's an architect.

8. a nurse
   Mary's a nurse.

9. a dentist
   Bob's a dentist.

≡ B.   Observe Occupations and Professions.

Teacher	Students
What am I?	You're a...(TEACHER)
What are you?	We're...(STUDENTS)
Picture 1. What is he?	1. He's a........(DOCTOR)
Picture 2. What is she?	2. She's a.......(SECRETARY)
Picture 3?	3. He's a........(CLERK)
Picture 4?	4. She's a.......(HOUSEWIFE)
Picture 5?	5. He's an.......(ENGINEER)
Picture 6?	6. He's a........(BUSINESSMAN)
Picture 7?	7. He's an.......(ARCHITECT)
Picture 8?	8. She's a.......(NURSE)
Picture 9?	9. He's a........(DENTIST)

Exercise 1.7 Practice Occupations and Professions. (Use the students'
names.)

Teacher	Student
1. What are you, Mr. A?	A. I'm a lawyer.
2. What are you, Miss B?	B. I'm a secretary.
3. Are you a doctor, Mr. C?	C. No, I'm a businessman.
4. Are you a businessman, Mr. D?	D. No, I'm a pharmacist.
5. Is Mr. D a dentist, Mr. E?	E. No, he's a pharmacist.
(Continue the exercise.)	

≡ C.   Observe WRONG, RIGHT, TIRED, HOMESICK, etc.

Teacher	Students
John says, "Detroit is in Texas."	He's ...(WRONG)
Mary says, "Detroit is in Michigan."	She's ...(RIGHT)
(Please look at the pictures)	
Picture 1. The doctor works very hard. It's now 5 p.m.	1. He's.....(TIRED)
Picture 2. The secretary is thinking about her family.	2. She's....(HOMESICK)
3. The clerk is very pleasant.	3. He's.....(NICE)
4. The housewife is working.	4. She's....(BUSY)
5. The engineer wants some water.	5. He's.....(THIRSTY)
6. The businessman wants some food.	6. He's.....(HUNGRY)
7. The architect wants to sleep.	7. He's.....(SLEEPY)
8. The nurse is smiling.	8. She's....(HAPPY)
9. The dentist is not smiling.	9. He's.....(SAD)

Exercise 1.8 Practice TIRED, HUNGRY, HAPPY, etc.

Examples: Teacher   Student

        Are you hungry, Mr. A?   A. Yes, I'm very hungry.
        Is Mr. A thirsty, Mr. B?   B. No, he's hungry.

1. Are you happy?   6. Is he busy?
2. Is he sad?   7. Is she nice?
3. Is he sleepy?   8. Is he right?
4. Are you tired?   9. Is he wrong?
5. Are you homesick?

Summary Dialogue. (Memorize.)

    Situation: Bill and Mary meet Mr. Taylor. Mary introduces Bill
           to Mr. Taylor.[1]

Mary: Mr. Taylor, this is Bill.

(Bill and Mr. Taylor shake hands.)

Bill: How do you do, Mr. Taylor.
Mr. Taylor: Hello, Bill. How are you?
Bill: Fine, thank you. Are you an architect, Mr. Taylor?
Mr. Taylor: (He shakes his head.) No, I'm not. I'm a teacher.
          What are you, Bill?

Bill: I'm an engineer.
Mr. Taylor: That's a good profession.
Bill: Thank you. Are you very busy now, Mr. Taylor?
Mr. Taylor: (He nods his head.) Yes, I am.

Bill: Well, good-bye. It was nice meeting you.
Mr. Taylor: Good-bye. Good-bye, Mary.

Homework.

Write a short conversation. Use the words and expressions in this
lesson.

NOTE TO TEACHER: [1]Introductions are taught in Lesson VIII.

Lesson II

A. AT, ON, IN with hour, day, month, year; IN THE morning; AT
   night.
B. Meals; WOULD LIKE, A CUP OF, etc.; PUT, STIR, etc.; SPOON,
   etc.
C. ALWAYS, USUALLY, OFTEN, etc.
D. WHAT KIND OF; LIKE, WANT.
E. HOW MUCH, TAX, CHANGE; Money.

Review Dialogue. (Memorize.)

    Situation: Bob leaves class. Mary drops her book.
             Bob picks up the book.

Bob: Excuse me, Mary. Is this your book?
Mary: Yes, it is. Thank you, Bob.
Bob: You're welcome. Is that a new pin?
Mary: Yes, it is. Do you like it?
Bob: Yes, I do. It's beautiful.
Mary: Thank you.
Bob: Are you busy now?
Mary: Yes, I have a class.
Bob: That's too bad. Good-bye.
Mary: Bye.

≡ A. 1   Observe AT, ON, IN with expressions of Time.

When did the students arrive?		
AT	8 o'clock	noon
	9:15	midnight
	5 p.m.	
ON	Sunday[1]	Thursday
	Monday	Friday
	Tuesday	Saturday
	Wednesday	
IN	January	July
	February	August
	March	September
	April	October
	May	November
	June	December
	1964	

NOTES: Use AT with hours, minutes ("points of time").
        Use ON with days (intermediate units of time).
        Use IN with years and months (large units of time).

NOTE TO TEACHER: [1]ON with dates is taught in Lesson IV.

Exercise 2.1   Practice IN, ON, AT with expressions of Time.

Examples: Teacher   Student

When did he arrive?   June   in June
                       Sunday   on Sunday
                       10 p.m.   at 10 p.m.

1. 1965	6. September	11. Tuesday
2. Saturday	7. noon	12. 1964
3. 3 o'clock	8. July	13. April
4. 4 p.m.	9. 10 a.m.	14. midnight
5. Monday	10. December	15. Friday

≡ A.2   Observe IN THE and AT in the following expressions.

Bill: What does Jack do?	
Sue: He has classes	IN THE MORNING,
he works	IN THE AFTERNOON,
he watches television	IN THE EVENING,
he eats lunch	AT NOON, and
he studies	AT NIGHT.

Exercise 2.2   Practice IN THE MORNING/AFTERNOON/EVENING
                and AT NOON/NIGHT.

Examples: Teacher   Student

When did she study?   night   at night
                       morning   in the morning

1. night	5. noon	9. morning
2. morning	6. afternoon	10. afternoon
3. afternoon	7. evening	11. noon
4. evening	8. night	12. evening

Exercise 2.3   Practice IN (THE), ON, AT with expressions of Time.

Examples: Teacher   Student

When did you arrive?   morning   in the morning
                        January   in January
                        3 p.m.   at 3 p.m.

1. Sunday	6. evening	11. February
2. afternoon	7. night	12. noon
3. 2 p.m.	8. March	13. Thursday
4. October	9. morning	14. 6 a.m.
5. midnight	10. 7 o'clock	15. night

☰ B.1   Observe Meals.

Bill: When do you eat?

Sue: I eat BREAKFAST at 7:30 a.m.,
                LUNCH   at noon, and
                DINNER   at 6 p.m.

NOTES: Use EAT or HAVE with BREAKFAST, LUNCH,
              DINNER, etc.
              DINNER is the main meal. (We often have dinner
              at noon on Sundays and holidays.)
              SUPPER indicates an evening meal.
              A SNACK is a light meal.

Exercise 2.4 Practice BREAKFAST, LUNCH, and DINNER.

Examples: Teacher   Student

What do you eat at 8 a.m.?   I eat breakfast at 8 a.m.
What do you eat at noon?   I eat lunch at noon.

1. at 7 a.m.   5. in the evening
2. at noon   6. at 12:15 p.m.
3. at night   7. at 6:30 p.m.
4. in the morning   8. at 1 p.m. on Sundays

☰ B.2   Observe WOULD LIKE; A CUP OF, A GLASS OF, etc.

        Teacher   Student

You are in a restaurant. What   I'D LIKE a glass of water.
   WOULD you LIKE?

- -

(Please look at the pictures, page 11.)

Picture 1. What would you like? I'd like. . .(A CUP OF coffee)
Picture 2. What would you like? I'd like. . .(A GLASS OF milk)
Picture 3?   I'd like. . .(A SLICE OF bread)
Picture 4?   I'd like. . .(A BOWL OF soup)
Picture 5?   I'd like. . .(A DISH OF ice cream)
Picture 6?   I'd like. . .(A PIECE OF pie)

NOTE: WOULD LIKE (I'D LIKE) is a polite form. It indicates
       desire, want.

Exercise 2.5   Practice WOULD LIKE (I'D LIKE).

Examples:	Teacher	Student
Picture 1.	What would you like, Mr. A?	A. I'd like a cup of coffee.
	Ask Mr. B.	A. What would you like, Mr. B?
Picture 2.		B. I'd like a glass of milk.
	Ask Mr. C.	B. What would you like, Mr. C?

1. Picture 3	5. Picture 2	9. Picture 3
2. Picture 4	6. Picture 6	10. Picture 4
3. Picture 5	7. Picture 1	
4. Picture 6	8. Picture 5	

≡ B.3   Observe PUT, STIR, EAT, CUT, DRINK; SPOON, KNIFE, FORK.

John: How does Bill eat dinner?

Mary: He PUTS the napkin on his lap,
he puts sugar in his coffee,
he STIRS the coffee with his SPOON,
he EATS his soup,
he CUTS a piece of meat with his KNIFE,
he eats his meat, salad, and vegetables with a FORK,
he DRINKS his coffee, and
he eats his dessert.

Exercise 2.6   Practice PUT, STIR, etc.; SPOON, etc.

Examples: <u>Teacher</u>   <u>Student</u>

Do you eat soup with a fork?   No, I eat soup with a spoon.
Do you put sugar in your soup?   No, I put sugar in my coffee.

1. Do you stir coffee with a knife?   6. Do you eat pie with a spoon?
2. Do you cut meat with a spoon?   7. Do you stir tea with a fork?
3. Do you eat salad with a spoon?   8. Do you drink soup?
4. Do you eat meat with a knife?   9. Do you eat milk?
5. Do you eat ice cream with a fork?   10. Do you put sugar in your milk?

≡ C. Observe ALWAYS, USUALLY, OFTEN, SOMETIMES, SELDOM, NEVER.[1]

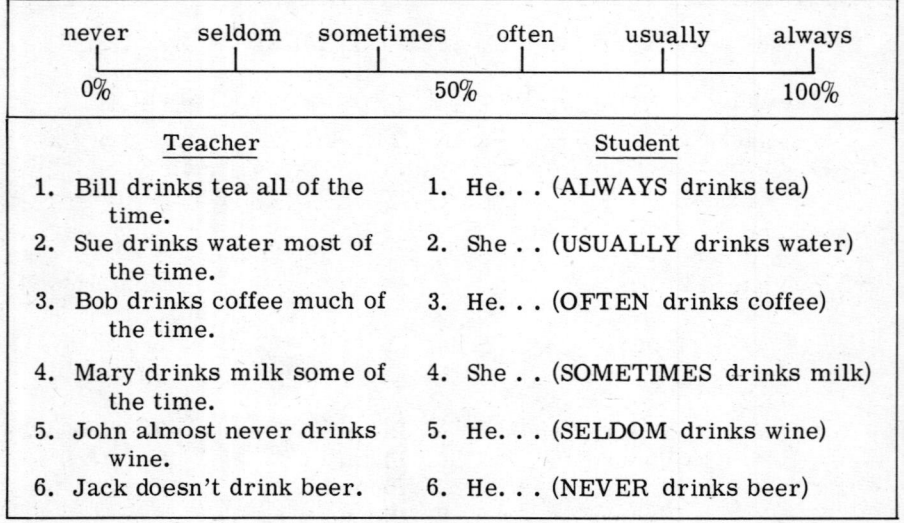

	Teacher		Student
1.	Bill drinks tea all of the time.	1.	He. . . (ALWAYS drinks tea)
2.	Sue drinks water most of the time.	2.	She . . (USUALLY drinks water)
3.	Bob drinks coffee much of the time.	3.	He. . . (OFTEN drinks coffee)
4.	Mary drinks milk some of the time.	4.	She . . (SOMETIMES drinks milk)
5.	John almost never drinks wine.	5.	He. . . (SELDOM drinks wine)
6.	Jack doesn't drink beer.	6.	He. . . (NEVER drinks beer)

Exercise 2.7   Practice ALWAYS, USUALLY, OFTEN, etc.

Examples: Teacher   Student

Jack studies all of the time.   He always studies.
He eats potatoes much of the time.   He often eats potatoes.

1. Bob has a large breakfast most of the time.
2. He eats lunch at twelve all of the time.
3. He almost never has dinner at eight.
4. Mary doesn't eat breakfast.
5. She has lunch at eleven much of the time.
6. She eats dinner at five some of the time.
7. She almost never eats dinner at eight.

NOTE TO TEACHER: [1] The scale may be put on the blackboard and filled in while presenting these items.

≡ D.   Observe WHAT KIND OF; LIKE, WANT.

Situation: Bob and Jack go to a restaurant.

> Bob: WHAT KIND OF ice cream do you LIKE?
> Jack: I LIKE chocolate ice cream.
>
> Bob: Do you LIKE ice cream cones?
> Jack: Yes, but I WANT a dish of ice cream today.

NOTES: LIKE indicates *general preference*.
        WANT indicates *desire*.

Exercise 2.8   Practice LIKE and WANT.

Examples:	Teacher		Student
	coffee	A.	Do you like coffee?
	tea	B.	Yes, but I want tea today.
	fish	C.	Do you like fish?
	steak	D.	Yes, but I want steak today.

1. coffee - milk
2. potatoes - rice
3. soup - salad
4. pie - fruit

5. beer - a coke
6. hot dogs - a hamburger
7. fried eggs - cereal
8. orange juice - tomato juice

≡ E.   Observe HOW MUCH, TAX, CHANGE, Money.

Situation: Bob and Jack finish their ice cream.

> Bob: Your ice cream is very good. HOW MUCH is a quart?[1]
> Waitress: Forty-nine cents and two cents TAX, fifty-one cents.
> -
> Bob: Do you have CHANGE for a TEN?
> Cashier: Yes. (He counts.) One FIVE, four ONES, a HALF-
>   DOLLAR, a QUARTER, a DIME, two NICKELS,
>   and five PENNIES. Is that all right?
>
> Bob: Yes, that's fine. Here is fifty-one cents.
> Cashier: Thank you.

NOTE TO TEACHER: [1]QUART and other measurements are taught in Lesson XV.

Exercise 2.9   Practice giving change.

Examples:	Teacher		Student
	a twenty-dollar bill	A.	Do you have change for a twenty-dollar bill?
		B.	Yes. I have two ten-dollar bills.
	a ten	C.	Do you have change for a ten?
		D.	Yes. I have two fives.

1. a five
2. a dollar
3. a half-dollar

4. a quarter
5. a dime
6. a nickel

Exercise 2.10   Practice PENNY, NICKEL, DIME, etc.

Examples: Teacher   Student

What kind of change do you have?   I have a quarter and two
(Write on board.) $ .45   dimes.
                        $6.36   I have a five, a one, a quarter
                                 two nickels, and a penny.

1. $3.17	4. $ 7.54	7. $156.00
2. $ .39	5. $15.15	8. $116.50
3. $1.90	6. $13.30	9. $ 11.11

Summary Dialogue. (Memorize.)

Situation: Jack and Sue are in a restaurant.

Jack: Did you arrive on Sunday?
Sue: Yes, I arrived at 6 o'clock in the morning.
Jack: When did John arrive?
Sue: He arrived at 3 in the afternoon.

(The waitress brings their dinner.)

Jack: Do you like the food?
Sue: Yes, it's very delicious.
Jack: What kind of dessert would you like?
Sue: I'd like a dish of ice cream.
Jack: Do you want a cup of coffee, too?
Sue: Yes, please.

Homework.

Write a short conversation. Use the words and expressions in this lesson.
Use Present time.

Lesson III

A. Numbers; ON with dates.
B. YESTERDAY, THIS, LAST, AGO.
C. EVERY, ALL.
D. WHAT TIME IS IT; EARLY, LATE, ON TIME.

Review Dialogue. (Memorize.)

Situation: Jack is in a restaurant. He speaks to the waiter.

Jack: What kind of pie do you have?
Waiter: Apple and lemon.
Jack: I'd like a piece of apple pie and a glass of milk.
Waiter: Here you are.
Jack: How much is it?
Waiter: Forty-two cents.

(Paul arrives. He orders a dish of chocolate ice cream and a
    cup of coffee.)

Jack: Paul, do you ever study at night?
Paul: Yes, sometimes; but not very often.
Jack: When do you study?
Paul: I usually study early in the morning.

A.1 Observe the Cardinal Numbers.

1	one	16	sixteen	101	one hundred one
2	two	17	seventeen		
3	three	18	eighteen	200	two hundred
4	four	19	nineteen	300	three hundred
5	five	20	twenty	400	four hundred
6	six			500	five hundred
7	seven	21	twenty-one	600	six hundred
8	eight			700	seven hundred
9	nine	30	thirty	800	eight hundred
10	ten	40	forty	900	nine hundred
		50	fifty	1,000	one thousand
11	eleven	60	sixty		
12	twelve	70	seventy	2,000	two thousand
13	thirteen	80	eighty		
14	fourteen	90	ninety	1,000,000	one million
15	fifteen	100	one hundred	2,000,000	two million

Exercise 3.1   Practice the Cardinal Numbers.

Examples: <u>Teacher</u>   <u>Student</u>

How much money did you have yesterday?
    (Write on board.) $100.00   I had one hundred dollars.
                         $ 15.50   I had fifteen dollars and
                                          fifty cents.

1. $ .16	6. $ 12.10	11. $ 1,234.56
2. $ .90	7. $ 118.29	12. $ 9,876.54
3. $ .76	8. $ 616.60	13. $ 10,017.70
4. $ .98	9. $ 904.02	14. $ 505,450.15
5. $5.48	10. $1,001.00	15. $1,000,000.00

≡ A.2a   Observe the Ordinal Numbers.

1st	first[1]	11th	eleventh
2nd	second[1]	12th	twelfth
3rd	third[1]	13th	thirteenth
4th	fourth	14th	fourteenth
5th	fifth	15th	fifteenth
6th	sixth	16th	sixteenth
7th	seventh		
8th	eighth	20th	twentieth
9th	ninth	21st	twenty-first
10th	tenth	22nd	twenty-second

≡ A.2b   Observe ON with Dates.

Review: Jack arrived at 8:30,
                    on Monday,
                    in January, 1963.

Secretary: When did you arrive?
Paul: I arrived ON JANUARY FOURTH.

Secretary: When is your birthday?
Paul: It's ON JULY TWENTY-FIRST.

NOTE TO TEACHER: [1] FIRST, SECOND, THIRD are irregular.

Exercise 3.2   Practice the Ordinal Numbers.

Examples: Teacher   Student

When did Paul arrive?
(Write on board.)   May 1   He arrived on May first.
                   June 2   He arrived on June second.

1.	Jan.	3	5.	May	14	9.	Sept.	23
2.	Feb.	5	6.	June	18	10.	Oct.	30
3.	March	9	7.	July	21	11.	Nov.	22
4.	April	7	8.	Aug.	31	12.	Dec.	6

Exercise 3.3   Practice Dates.

          Teacher   Student

When is your birthday, Mr. A?   A.   My birthday is on May third.
    Ask Mr. B.   A.   When's your birthday, Mr. B?
                          B.   My birthday's on June fifth.
(Continue the exercise.)   B.   When's your birthday, Miss C?

≡ B.1   Observe YESTERDAY and LAST.

Mary: What did Paul do yesterday?

Sue: He attended class   YESTERDAY MORNING,
         practiced English   YESTERDAY NOON,
         played tennis   YESTERDAY AFTERNOON,
         did his homework   YESTERDAY EVENING, and

         visited his friend   LAST NIGHT.

Exercise 3.4   Practice YESTERDAY MORNING, LAST NIGHT, etc.

Examples: Teacher   Student

When did Paul study?   morning   He studied yesterday morning.
                  night   He studied last night.

1.	afternoon	4.	noon
2.	night	5.	evening
3.	morning	6.	night

≡ B.2   Observe THIS and TO-.

Situation: It's 11:30 p.m.

Mary: When did Marie arrive?
Sue: She arrived THIS MORNING.
Mary: What did she do TODAY?

Sue: She studied vocabulary   THIS NOON,
            attended class   THIS AFTERNOON, and
            visited friends   THIS EVENING.

Mary: Was she tired TONIGHT?
Sue: Yes, she was very tired.

Exercise 3.5   Practice THIS MORNING, TODAY, etc.

Examples: Teacher   Student

When was Marie tired? morning   She was tired this morning.
                       night   She was tired tonight.
                       day   She was tired today.

1. afternoon   4. morning
2. noon   5. evening
3. night   6. day

≡ B.3   Observe LAST and THIS.

Situation: It's Saturday morning.

Bill: Don't you like cold weather?
Mary: No, I don't. I like hot weather.

Bill: It was hot LAST MONTH.
Mary: Yes, but it was cold THIS MONTH.

Bill: LAST WEEK was warm.
Mary: Yes, but THIS WEEK was very cool.

NOTES: LAST indicates the PRECEDING week, month, etc.
        THIS indicates the PRESENT week, month, etc.

Exercise 3.6   Practice LAST and THIS.

Situation: Today is Friday, September 19.[1]

```
┌─────────────────────────────────────┐
│           SEPTEMBER                  │
│   S    M    T    W   Th    F    S    │
│   7    8    9   10   11   12   13    │
│  14   15   16   17   18  (19)   --   │
└─────────────────────────────────────┘
```

Examples: Teacher   Student

When was the weather hot?
    in August   It was hot last month.
    on September 10, 11, 12   It was hot last week.
    on Thursday, September 11   It was hot last Thursday.

1. in September   5. on September 11, 12, 13
2. on September 15, 16, 17   6. on Wednesday, September 17
3. on September 8, 9, 10   7. on Friday, September 12
4. in August   8. on Saturday, September 13

Ξ B.4   Observe AGO.

Situation: It's Friday evening.

```
┌──────────────────────────────────────────────────────────┐
│ Marie:  When did you arrive here, Mary?                    │
│ Mary:   Last Saturday afternoon.                           │
│ Marie:  That was SIX DAYS AGO.                             │
│                                                            │
│ Mary:   Yes, that's right.  You arrived TWELVE HOURS AGO,  │
│                  I arrived A WEEK AGO, and                 │
│                  Bill arrived TWO MONTHS AGO.              │
└──────────────────────────────────────────────────────────┘
```

Exercise 3.7   Practice AGO.

Examples: Teacher   Student

It's 9 a.m. I arrived at 6 a.m.   You arrived three hours ago.

It's 1965. I arrived in 1963.   You arrived two years ago.

   1.   It's Saturday. I arrived on Thursday.
   2.   It's February. I arrived in December.
   3.   It's 11 o'clock. I arrived at 9 o'clock.
   4.   It's 1958. I arrived in 1954.
   5.   It's August. I arrived in May.
   6.   It's 10:15. I arrived at 10.
   7.   It's 1964. I arrived in 1959.
   8.   It's July 13th. I arrived on June 30th.

NOTE TO TEACHER: [1]Put calendar on blackboard.

☰ C.1   Observe EVERY.

> Bob: Did you study last week, Paul?
> Paul: Yes, I studied EVERY day. I studied on Sunday,
>   Monday, Tuesday, Wednesday, Thursday,
>   Friday, and Saturday.
>
> Bob: Did you practice your lessons every night?
> Paul: Yes, I always practiced them at night.
>
> Bob: When do you play tennis?
> Paul: Every Friday afternoon.

NOTE: EVERY indicates repeated or customary action.

Exercise 3.8   Practice EVERY.

Examples: Teacher   Student

Mary studied on S, M, T, W, Th, F, & S.   She studied every day.
She was always happy in the morning.   She was happy every
                                             morning.

1. She studied at night on S, M, T, W, Th, F, and S.
2. She studied at 4 in the afternoon on S, M, T, W, Th, F, and S.
3. Paul always wanted two cups of coffee in the morning.
4. He always wanted a glass of tea in the afternoon.
5. He always wanted a dish of ice cream at night.
6. Sue always watched television on Saturday night.
7. She always attended church on Sunday.
8. John and Bob were always tired on Monday morning.
9. They were always happy on Friday afternoon.

☰ C.2   Observe ALL.

Situation: It's afternoon.

> Paul: Did you work from eight to twelve this morning?
> Bob: Yes, I worked ALL morning. We were very busy.
> Paul: I was tired this morning. I worked all day yesterday.

NOTE: ALL indicates an entire period of time.

Exercise 3.9   Practice ALL.

Example: <u>Teacher</u>   <u>Student</u>

     Bob worked from eight to twelve.   He worked all morning.

1. He studied grammar from noon to six.
2. He practiced English from six to midnight.
3. He repeated the words from eight to noon yesterday.
4. He was busy from noon to five yesterday.
5. He was homesick from Sunday to Saturday.

☰ D.1   Observe Time Expressions:

Situation: It's Saturday.

Jim:	What time is it?
Bill:	It's five o'clock (5:00).
Jim:	What did you do before[1] lunch?
Bill:	I listened to the radio at EIGHT FIFTEEN (8:15), washed my clothes at NINE THIRTY (9:30), and walked downtown at TEN FORTY-FIVE (10:45).
Jim:	What did you do after[1] lunch?
Bill:	I waited for a bus at A QUARTER AFTER ONE (1:15), opened my window at HALF PAST TWO (2:30), and closed the window at A QUARTER TO THREE (2:45).

Exercise 3.10   Practice the time pattern HOURS:MINUTES.

Examples: <u>Teacher</u>   <u>Student</u>

    What time is it?   7:05   It's seven five.
    (Write on board.) 8:30   It's eight thirty.
                    2:58   It's two fifty-eight.

1. 8:55   4. 6:02   7. 3:30
2. 5:20   5. 9:45   8. 3:50
3. 1:10   6. 11:00   9. 2:10

NOTE TO TEACHER: [1]BEFORE and AFTER are taught in Lesson XVI.

≡ D.2   Observe EARLY, ON TIME, LATE.

> Paul: Were you LATE to class this morning?
> Jim: No, I was ON TIME. I arrived at eight sharp.
>
> Paul: Was the teacher EARLY?
> Jim: Yes, he came at seven fifty-five.

Exercise 3.11   Practice EARLY, LATE, ON TIME.

Examples: <u>Teacher</u>   <u>Student</u>

The movies begin at 7 o'clock sharp every night.
    Bill arrived at 7:05 yesterday.   Bill was 5 minutes late.
    Mary arrived at 6:55.   Mary was 5 minutes early.
    Bob arrived at 7 sharp.   Bob was on time.

1.   We eat lunch at 12 noon every day.

    a.   John arrived at twelve fifteen yesterday.
    b.   Helen arrived at eleven fifty.
    c.   Bill arrived at twelve one.

2.   The course begins on February 2nd every year.

    a.   Bob arrived on January 2nd last year.
    b.   Sue arrived on February 3rd.
    c.   Paul arrived on February 2nd.

Summary Dialogue. (Memorize.)

    Situation: Today is June 13.

    Jim: When did you arrive, Bill?
    Bill: I arrived a week ago.

    Jim: What day was it?[1]
    Bill: It was June fifth. When did you arrive?[1]

    Jim: I arrived on June fourth.
    Bill: Did you arrive at night?

    Jim: No, I arrived at four thirty in the morning.
    Bill: I arrived at ten fifteen at night.

Homework.

    Write a short conversation. Use the words and expressions in this
lesson. Use Past time.

NOTE TO TEACHER: [1] Note the contrast: "What day? . . June 5."
"When? . . On June 4."

Lesson IV

A. AT, ON, IN: *addresses;* AT, IN: *location.*
B. TO THE store, TO school, home.
C. WHO, WHAT, WHICH, WHEN, WHERE.
D. NEAR, FAR FROM; THE NEXT evening.
E. DRUGSTORE, BANK, LIBRARY, etc.
F. EXPENSIVE, WIDE, FAST, OLD, SHORT, etc.

Review Dialogue. (Memorize.)

Jim studied very hard last night. He practiced all of the words and all of the patterns in Lesson III.

It's morning now. Jim and Bill are in the classroom.

Bill: Do you study every night, Jim?
Jim: No, I sometimes visit friends.
Bill: Are you tired this morning?
Jim: Yes, a little.
Bill: What time is it?
Jim: It's eight o'clock sharp. We're ten minutes early.

☰ A.1   Observe AT, ON, IN: *addresses.*

Paul:	Where does John live now?		
Bill:	He lives	AT	612 STATE STREET.
		AT	515 CENTRAL AVENUE.
	He lives	ON	STATE STREET.
		ON	CENTRAL AVENUE.
	He lives	IN	THE UNITED STATES.
		IN	MICHIGAN.
		IN	DETROIT.

NOTES: Use AT with house NUMBERS.
Use ON with street NAMES.
Use IN with cities, states, countries.

23

Exercise 4.1   Practice addresses.

Examples: Teacher   Student

Where does Mary live now?
     Ann Arbor   She lives in Ann Arbor.
     State Street   She lives on State Street.
     here   She lives here.

1. Michigan   6. State Street
2. New York   7. 313 State Street
3. 324 State Street   8. Mexico
4. Main Street   9. Madison Avenue
5. 768 Central Avenue   10. Detroit

☰ A.2   Observe AT: *location.*

Marie:	What was Helen doing today?
Sue:	She was teaching AT THE UNIVERSITY at ten thirty, reading AT THE LIBRARY at eleven thirty, eating AT A RESTAURANT at twelve thirty, and working AT HOME at one thirty.

NOTE: The emphasis is on a POINT.

Exercise 4.2   Practice AT: *location.*

Examples: Teacher   Student

What is Helen doing now?
    teach . . . the university   She's teaching at the university.
    work . . . home   She's working at home.

1. study . . . the library   6. eat breakfast . . . the restaurant
2. study Lesson 3 . . . home   7. arrive . . . the airport
3. teach English . . . the university 8. play tennis . . . school
4. learn French . . . school   9. eat lunch . . . the university
5. eat dinner . . . home   10. practice English . . . home

☰ A.3   Observe IN: *location.*

> | John: | What was Bob doing today? |
> |---|---|
> | Jack: | He was teaching IN THE UNIVERSITY at ten fifteen, reading IN THE LIBRARY at eleven fifteen, and eating IN THE RESTAURANT at twelve fifteen. |

NOTE: The emphasis is on the INTERIOR of a place or thing.

Exercise 4.3   Practice IN: *location.*

Examples: <u>Teacher</u>   <u>Student</u>

What is Bob doing now?
    teach . . . the university   He's teaching in the university.
    drink tea . . . the restaurant   He's drinking tea in the restaurant.
    read a book . . . the park   He's reading a book in the park.

1. study . . . the language laboratory
2. play tennis . . . the park
3. teach . . . the university
4. eat dinner . . . the dormitory
5. drink coffee . . . the restaurant
6. eat lunch . . . the cafeteria
7. do his homework . . . the library
8. play ping-pong . . . the dormitory
9. read a newspaper . . . the library
10. practice English . . . the bookstore

☰ B.   Observe TO.

> | Jim: | Where're you going? | | |
> |---|---|---|---|
> | Bill: | I'm going | TO THE | STORE. |
> | | | TO THE | BANK. |
> | | | TO THE | MOVIES. |
> | | I'm going | TO | DETROIT. |
> | | | TO | WARD'S. |
> | | I'm going | TO | CLASS. |
> | | | TO | CHURCH. |
> | | | TO . | SCHOOL. |
> | | I'm going | | HOME. |
> | | | | DOWNTOWN. |

NOTES: With actions like GO, use TO (THE) before expressions of
       place. TO CLASS, TO CHURCH, TO SCHOOL, HOME, and
       DOWNTOWN are special expressions.

Exercise 4.4   Practice TO.

Examples: Teacher   Student

Situation: We meet at the bus stop.
Where are you going, Mr. A? home   A. I'm going home.
Ask Mr. B.   A. Where are you
                                         going, Mr. B?

                          bookstore B. I'm going to the
Ask Mr. C.   bookstore. Where
                                         are you going, Mr. C?

1. Chicago	5. New York	9. class
2. bank	6. school	10. store
3. church	7. home	11. downtown
4. restaurant	8. post office	12. Ward's

≡ C.   Observe WHO, WHAT, WHICH, WHERE, WHEN.

Situation: Tom learned his grammar lesson in class today.

		QUESTION WORD	REFERS TO
Helen:	Who did what?	who	a person
Jack:	Tom learned his lesson.	what	a thing
Helen:	Which lesson?	which	a specific thing
Jack:	His grammar lesson.		or person
Helen:	When and where?	when	a time
Jack:	Today. In class.	where	a place

Exercise 4.5   Practice WHO, WHAT, WHICH, WHEN, WHERE.

            Teacher   Student

a) Bill studies his vocabulary book
      at home every night.

    Who does what?   Bill studies his book.

1. What does Bill do?	4. Who studies?
2. Where does he do it?	5. Which book does he study?
3. When does he do it?	6. Where and when does he do it?

b) The pronunciation teacher is
      eating lunch there now.

1. What is he doing?	4. When is he doing it?
2. Who's eating lunch?	5. Where is he doing it?
3. Which teacher?	6. Who's doing what, where, and when?

≡ D. Observe NEAR, FAR FROM; THE NEXT evening.

Situation: It's Saturday. Helen and her brother are in Miami.

Helen:	Were you NEAR Detroit last Tuesday evening?
Tom:	No, I was attending a concert in Chicago.
Helen:	That's not very FAR FROM Detroit.
Tom:	Yes, it is. It's three hundred miles.
Helen:	Where were you THE NEXT[1] evening?
Tom:	Wednesday evening? I was here in Miami.

Exercise 4.6   Practice NEAR and FAR FROM.

Examples: Teacher   Student

Are we near Chicago, Mr. A?   A. No, we're far from Chicago.
Are you far from the door,   B. No, I'm near the door.
    Mr. B?

1. Is Mr. B near the window?   6. Are they far from us?
2. Are we far from Detroit?   7. Am I near you, Mr. C?
3. Are we near New York City?   8. Are you near him, Miss D?
4. Are you far from me?   9. Are you near her, Mr. E?
5. Are we far from them?   10. Is he far from her, Mr. F?
                                 11. Is she near him, Mrs. G?

≡ E.   Observe DRUGSTORE, BANK, LIBRARY, etc.

Situation: Bob meets John on Washington Avenue.

Bob: Hi, John. Where are you going?
John: Hello, Bob.

I'm going to		WOOLWORTH'S	for some . . . (shoestrings)
	to the	DRUGSTORE	for some . . . (medicine)
	to the	GROCERY STORE	for some . . . (milk and bread)
	to the	CLOTHING STORE	for some . . . (new socks)
	to the	SHOESTORE	for some . . . (new shoes)
	to the	DEPARTMENT STORE	for a . . . . . . (key and an iron)
	to the	BOOKSTORE	for some . . . (books)
I'm going	to the	BARBERSHOP	for a . . . . . . (haircut)
	to the	POST OFFICE	for some . . . (stamps)
	to the	BANK	for some . . . (money)
	to the	LAUNDRY	for my . . . . (shirts)
	to the	(DRY) CLEANERS	for my . . . . (suit)
	to the	LIBRARY	for a . . . . . . (book)

NOTE TO TEACHER: [1]NEXT indicates a sequence of events here;
NEXT as a future time expression is taught in Lesson V.

Exercise 4.7   Practice DRUGSTORE, BANK, LIBRARY, etc.

Examples: <u>Teacher</u>   <u>Student</u>

a) Where is John going?
    He needs some money.   He's going to the bank.
    He needs some shoestrings. He's going to Woolworth's.
    He needs some bread.   He's going to the grocery store.

1. a haircut	4. some money	7. a new shirt
2. his suit	5. some shoe polish	8. some milk
3. some stamps	6. a book	9. some medicine

b) Is he going to the <u>bank</u> for a   No, he's going to the drugstore.
    toothbrush?

1. . . . to the <u>library</u> for an apple?   5. . . . to the <u>shoestore</u> for
                                                       a pencil?
2. . . . to the <u>laundry</u> for an   6. . . . to the <u>barbershop</u> for
   umbrella?   a comb?
3. . . . to the <u>post office</u> for a   7. . . . to the <u>grocery store</u>
   hairbrush?   for a key?
4. . . . to the <u>clothing store</u> for an   8. . . . to the <u>clothing store</u>
   iron?   for a watch?

≡ F.1   Observe EXPENSIVE, WIDE, HIGH, etc.

1. This suit costs $200.	1. It's . . . (EXPENSIVE)
2. That suit costs $ 20.	2. It's . . . (CHEAP)
3. Main Street has four lanes.	3. It's . . . (WIDE)
4. State Street has two lanes.	4. It's . . . (NARROW)
5. The temperature is ninety degrees.	5. It's . . . (HIGH)
6. The temperature is thirty degrees.	6. It's . . . (LOW)
7. Mr. Harris is in the hospital.	7. He's . . . (SICK)
8. Mrs. Gray is not in the hospital.	8. She's . . . (WELL)
9. New York has 8 million people.	9. It's . . . (LARGE)
10. Albany has 30,000 people.	10. It's . . . (SMALL)
11. A plane goes 600 miles per hour.	11. It's . . . (FAST)
12. My car goes 35 miles per hour.	12. It's . . . (SLOW)

Exercise 4.8   Practice EXPENSIVE, WIDE, HIGH, etc.

Examples: Teacher   Student

Is a bicycle fast?   No, it's slow.
Was that book cheap?   No, it was expensive.

1. Is Tokyo small?   5. Is 32° Fahrenheit high?
2. Is Main Street wide?   6. Is a jet plane slow?
3. Are we sick?   7. Is our city large?
4. Is 32° Centigrade high?   8. Are these small books expensive?

Ξ F.2   Observe TALL, YOUNG, HEAVY, etc.

A TALL

YOUNG man

was buying a LONG key-chain

and a NEW car.

A SHORT

OLD man

was buying a SHORT key-chain

and an OLD car.

The young man is mailing
  a HEAVY package.
He is wearing
  a DARK BLUE shirt.

The old man is mailing
  a LIGHT package.
He is wearing
  a LIGHT BLUE shirt.
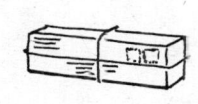

Exercise 4.9   Practice TALL, YOUNG, etc. (Please look at the pictures.)

Examples: Teacher   Student

Was the young man buying an old car?   No, he was buying a new car.
Is the old man wearing a light shirt?   Yes, he is wearing a light shirt.

1. What was the young man buying?   7. Was the young man short?
2. What was the old man buying?   8. Was the short man young?
3. What is the young man mailing?   9. Is the young man mailing a
4. What is the old man mailing?   light package?
5. What is the young man wearing?   10. Is the old man wearing a dark
6. What is the old man wearing?   shirt?

☰ F.3   Observe EASY, HARD, SOFT, LOUD

Jack likes EASY problems, a SOFT bed, and SOFT music.	$\begin{array}{r} 1 \\ +1 \\ \hline 2 \end{array}$		

Bob likes HARD problems, a HARD bed, and LOUD music.	$x^2 = -20$		

Exercise 4.10   Practice EASY, HARD, SOFT, LOUD. (Please look at the pictures.)

Example: <u>Teacher</u>   <u>Student</u>

Is "1 + 1 = 2" a hard problem?   No, it's an easy problem.

1. What does Jack like?   5. Does Bob like easy problems?
2. What does Bob like?   6. What kind of bed does Jack like?
3. Does Jack like loud music?   7. Is "X^2 = -20" an easy problem?
4. Does Bob like soft music?   8. Does Bob like violin music or
                                         drum music?

Summary Dialogue. (Memorize.)

    Situation: Tom meets Helen.

    Tom: Where are you going, Helen?
    Helen: I'm going to the Tower Hotel.

    Tom: Are you living there now?
    Helen: No, I'm living in a dormitory this year.

    Tom: What are you studying at the university?
    Helen: I'm studying French and Spanish.

Homework.

Write a short conversation. Use some of the words and expressions in this lesson. Use BE with -ing.

Lesson V

A. TOMORROW, NEXT, FROM NOW.
B. BOTTLE, TUBE, PACKAGE, etc.
C. IN, BESIDE, BELOW, etc.
D. DORMITORY, BOARDING HOUSE, etc.

Review Dialogue. (Memorize.)

Susan lives in a dormitory on Central Avenue.

She teaches English at Lincoln School every morning at nine. She studies French at the university every afternoon. She studies all afternoon.

Yesterday, she ate dinner at Smith's Cafe. James was there, too.

James: Do you often eat at this restaurant, Susan?
Susan: Yes. I like the food here very much.
James: This steak dinner is certainly good.
Susan: It's cheap, too.
James: Yes, it is. Would you like a glass of water?
Susan: No, thank you.

≡ A.1 Observe TOMORROW.

James: What are you going to do TOMORROW?

Susan: I'm going to study   TOMORROW MORNING,
        write letters   TOMORROW NOON,
        walk downtown   TOMORROW AFTERNOON, and
        do my homework   TOMORROW EVENING.

James: What are you going to do TOMORROW NIGHT?
Susan: I'm going to visit some friends.

Exercise 5.1   Practice TOMORROW MORNING, etc.

Examples: Teacher   Student

When is Susan going to study?
    10 a.m., tomorrow   She's going to study tomorrow morning.
    11 p.m.   She's going to study tomorrow night.

    1. 2 p.m.   3. 7 p.m.   5. 4:15 p.m.
    2. 11:59 a.m.   4. 11:30 a.m.   6. 10:45 p.m.

Exercise 5.2   Describe James' activities.[1]

TOMORROW					
9 a.m.	11 a.m.	12 noon	3 p.m.	7 p.m.	10 p.m.
study vocabulary	telephone Susan	eat lunch	play ping-pong	visit a friend	do his homework

Examples: Teacher   Student
    What is James going to do tomorrow?
        at 9 a.m.   He's going to study vocabulary at
                            9 a.m.
        at 11 a.m.   He's going to telephone Susan at
                            11 a.m.

1. at 12 noon   5. at 9 a.m. and at 12 noon
2. at 3 p.m.   6. at 3 p.m. and at 7 p.m.
3. at 7 p.m.   7. at 11 a.m. and at 3 p.m.
4. at 10 p.m.   8. at 12 noon, 7 p.m. and 10 p.m.

≡ A.2   Observe NEXT.

> Joe: What are you going to do NEXT WEEK, Don?
>
> Don: I studied last week,
>   I'm studying this week, and
>   I'm going to study NEXT WEEK, too.

NOTE: NEXT indicates future time.

Exercise 5.3   Practice NEXT.

    Situation: Today is Friday, September 19.

SEPTEMBER						
S	M	T	W	T	F	S
--	--	--	--	--	(19)	20
21	22	23	24	25	26	27

Examples: Teacher   Student
    When are you going downtown?
        week   I'm going downtown next week.
        at 4 p.m., Wednesday I'm going downtown next Wednesday
                             afternoon.

1. on Monday   5. at 9 a.m., Tuesday
2. on Sunday, September 21 6. at 8 p.m., Thursday
3. in October   7. at 11 p.m., Monday
4. on Friday, September 26 8. at 3 p.m., Saturday, Sept. 27

NOTE TO TEACHER: [1]Put diagram on blackboard. Exercise 5.2 gives
practice in the production of long sentences.

≡ A.3   Observe FROM NOW, IN. . . MINUTES.

Situation: It's 5:30 Friday Afternoon.

Joe:	What are you going to do during[1] the weekend?
James:	I'm going to go to Detroit. What are you going to do?
Joe:	I'm going to go to Niagara Falls. My bus leaves IN FIFTEEN MINUTES.
James:	When are you coming back?
Joe:	TWO DAYS FROM NOW.
James:	Have a good time!
Joe:	Thank you.

Exercise 5.4   Practice FROM NOW.

Examples:	Teacher	Student
	It's 7 a.m. Susan's going to be here at 7:20.	She's going to be here 20 minutes from now.
	It's 1962. She's going to be here in 1963.	She's going to be here a year from now.

1. It's May 10. She's going to be here on May 17.
2. It's 5. She's going to be here at 8:30.
3. It's Thursday. She's going to be here on Sunday.
4. It's March. She's going to be here in April.
5. It's August. She's going to be here in November.
6. It's Tuesday. She's going to be here on Saturday.
7. It's 11 a.m. She's going to be here at 4 p.m.
8. It's Wednesday. She's going to be here next Wednesday.

≡ B.   Observe BOTTLE, TUBE, PACKAGE, etc.

Situation: Don is in White's Drugstore.

Clerk:	May I help you?		
Don:	Yes, please. I'd like	A BOTTLE	OF blue ink.
		A TUBE	OF toothpaste.
		A PACKAGE	OF razor blades.
		A BOX	OF Kleenex.
		A CAN	OF shaving cream.
	I'd also like	A BAR	OF soap.
		A ROLL	OF film.
		A PACK	OF cigarettes.
		A BOOK	OF matches.
		A BALL	OF string.

NOTE TO TEACHER: [1]DURING is taught in Lesson XVI.

Exercise 5.5   Practice BOTTLE, TUBE, PACKAGE, etc.

Examples: <u>Teacher</u>   <u>Student</u>

What is Don going to buy?
   blue ink   He's going to buy a bottle of blue ink.
   film   He's going to buy a roll of film.

1. razor blades	6. toothpaste
2. matches	7. cigarettes
3. string	8. blue ink
4. Kleenex	9. soap
5. shaving cream	10. film

☰ C.   Observe IN, BESIDE, BELOW, etc.

Situation: Jim is studying in his room.

(Please look at the picture.)

Teacher	Student
1. Where is Jim?	1. He's . . . (AT the desk)
2. Where is Jim?	2. He's . . . (INSIDE the room)
3. Where is the tree?	3. It's . . . . (OUTSIDE the room)
4. Where is the map?	4. It's . . . . (ON the wall)
5. Where is the clock?	5. It's . . . . (ON the chest)
6. Where is the waste-basket?	6. It's . . . . (BESIDE the desk)
7. Where is the light?	7. It's . . . . (ABOVE the desk)
8. Where is the desk?	8. It's . . . . (BELOW the light)
9. Where are Joe's legs?	9. They're . (UNDER the desk)
10. Where is the bed?	10. It's . . . . (IN BACK OF Joe)
11. Where is the armchair?	11. It's . . . . (IN FRONT OF the bookcase)
12. Where is the chest?	12. It's . . . . (BETWEEN the bed and the bookcase)

Exercise 5.6   Practice IN, ON, BESIDE, etc.

    Examples: Teacher   Student

        Is Jim on the desk?   No, Jim is at the desk.
        Is the rug in the floor?   No, the rug is on the floor.
        Are Jim's legs in the desk? No, Jim's legs are under the desk.

1. Is the calendar below the map?
2. Are the books on the bookcase?
3. Is Jim in the desk?
4. Is the table on the hall?
5. Is the wastebasket between the desk?
6. Is the blanket in the bed?
7. Is the telephone inside the room?
8. Is the armchair in back of the bookcase?
9. Is the clock in the chest?
10. Is the tree inside the room?
11. Is the calendar in the wall?
12. Is the desk above the light?
13. Is the bookcase in front of the armchair?
14. Are the papers in the rug?
15. Is the picture below the book-case?
16. Is the chest in back of the bookcase and the bed?

Exercise 5.7   Practice IN, ON, BESIDE, etc.

    Examples: Teacher   Student

    Where's your book?   the floor   My book's on the floor.
    Where's the table?   the light   The table's below the light.

1. Where's the blackboard? the wall
2. Where are we? the room
3. Where's Mr. A? Miss B
4. Where's Miss B? the teacher
5. Where's Mrs. C? Mr. D and Mr. E
6. Where's the tree? the room
7. Where's the light? the table
8. Where's the book? the desk
9. Where are you? the light
10. Where's the blackboard? the table

≡ D.   Observe DORMITORY, BOARDING HOUSE, etc.

Situation:. Don and Joe are roommates.

Don: Are you going to live in the DORMITORY next semester, Joe?
Joe: No, I don't think so. I'm going to look at some APARTMENTS day after tomorrow.

Don: I looked at a BOARDING HOUSE, a room in a PRIVATE HOME, and a CO-OP day before yesterday.

Joe: What's a boarding house?
Don: It's like a restaurant. You[1] only eat there.

Joe: Where do you sleep?
Don: You usually sleep in a ROOMING HOUSE or in a room in a private home.

Joe: How is a Co-op different?
Don: A Co-op is like a dormitory; you eat and sleep there. It's not very expensive because every person washes dishes and works.

NOTE TO TEACHER: [1]Note the nonpersonal use of YOU, meaning "any person."

Exercise 5.8   Please answer the questions.

1. What is a boarding house?
2. What is a rooming house?
3. What does "room and board" mean?
4. Is a Co-op expensive?
5. How do you pay for room and board in a Co-op?

Summary Dialogue. (Memorize.)

Situation: It's night. We're at a party in New York. Susan is
            talking to Mary.

Susan: Helen went to Boston last week. She directed a program
        there the night before last. She came to New York the
        next morning.

Mary: I saw her during our program yesterday. She likes New York
       very much. She has many friends here.

(Helen joins them.)

Susan: Helen, are you going to be here for the next three weeks?
Helen: No, I don't think so. I'm going to go to San Francisco the
        week after next.

Susan: What are you going to do during these two weeks?
Helen: I'm going to visit my friends, listen to some lectures, and
        look at some art exhibits.

Susan: You're going to be very busy.
Helen: I always am.

Homework.

Write a short conversation. Use some of the words and expressions
in this lesson. Use Future time.

Lesson VI

A. The Human Body; SEE, HEAR, SMELL, etc.
B. WEAR, Clothing, Colors.
C. A FEW, A LITTLE, A LOT OF, MUCH, MANY, SEVERAL.
D. MISS, LOSE, WASTE.
E. AS FAR AS, UNTIL.

Review Dialogue.[1]

Teacher: Are the books in the desk or on the desk?
Student: Both. One book is in the desk and one is on the desk.

Teacher: Does a person ever sit in a table?
Student: No. He always sits at a table.

Teacher: Doesn't he sometimes sit on a table?
Student: Yes, but very seldom.

☰ A.1   Observe the words for parts of the Body.[2]

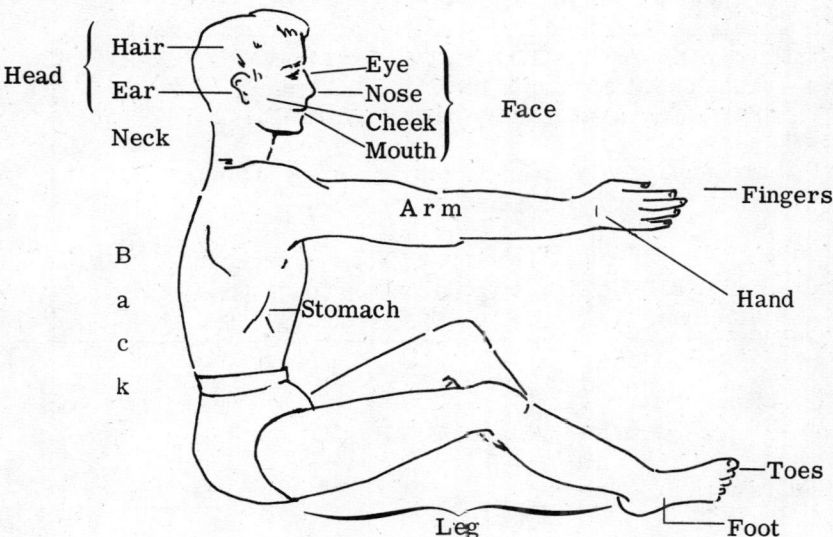

NOTE: The parts of the MOUTH are the LIPS, the TEETH, and the
       TONGUE.

NOTES TO TEACHER: [1]Refer to a picture of a desk. (See Lesson X.)
    [2] Additional items for advanced classes: forehead, chin, shoulder,
elbow, wrist, fingernail, chest, waist, hip, knee, ankle, toenail.

Exercise 6.1   Practice HEAD, FOOT, NOSE, etc.

Examples: <u>Teacher</u>   <u>Student</u>

(touching his head)   Is this my arm?   No, it's your head.
(showing his fingers)   Are these my toes?   No, they're your fingers.
(pointing at his nose)   Is this my nose?   Yes, it is.

1. (ear) Is this my eye?   6. (cheek) Is this my cheek?
2. (stomach) Is this my back?   7. (foot) Is that my leg?
3. (teeth) Are these my toes?   8. (mouth) Is this my mouth?
4. (toes) Are those my toes?   9. (lips) Are these my teeth?
5. (hand) Is this my arm?   10. (head) Is this my leg?

≡ A.2   Observe TOUCH, HEAR, SEE, etc.

Situation: Paul is telling a story.

This morning a hand TOUCHED me and I HEARD, ''Paul,
wake up. It's time for class.'' I opened my eyes and
SAW several students. They all LAUGHED.

My roommate said, ''Good morning. Are you going to
sleep all day? Here's some breakfast.''

I SMILED and said, ''Thank you. You are very kind.'' The
coffee SMELLED very good and the doughnuts TASTED
excellent.

Exercise 6.2   Practice TOUCH, HEAR, SEE, etc.

Examples: <u>Teacher</u>   <u>Student</u>

Did an arm touch Paul?   No, it was a hand.
Does Paul hear with his eyes?   No, he hears with his ears.
Do you see with your ears?   No, I see with my eyes.

1. Do you laugh with your hands?   6. Do you touch with your fingers?
2. Do you smile with your ears?   7. Do you hear with your nose?
3. Do you smell with your cheek?   8. Do you walk with your arms?
4. Do you taste with your tongue?   9. Do you taste with your fingers?
5. Do you see with your arms?   10. Do you touch with your toes?

≡ B.1   Observe WEAR and Clothing.

> Teacher: What am I WEARING?
> Student: You're wearing a SUIT, a SHIRT, a TIE, SHOES, SOCKS,
>   GLASSES, and a WRISTWATCH.
>
> (Please look at the pictures, page 40.)
>
> | Teacher | Student |
> |---|---|
> | Picture 1. What is John wearing? | 1. He's wearing...(a SUIT) |
> | Picture 2? | 2. He's wearing...(a SHIRT) |
> | Picture 3? | 3. He's wearing...(SLACKS) |
> | Picture 4? | 4. He's wearing...(a SPORT JACKET) |
> | Picture 5? | 5. He's wearing...(a HAT) |
> | Picture 6? | 6. He's wearing...(SLIPPERS) |
> | Picture 7? | 7. He's wearing...(a TIE) |
> | Picture 8? | 8. He's wearing...(PAJAMAS) |
> | Picture 9. What is Mary wearing? | 9. She's wearing...(a SUIT) |
> | Picture 10? | 10. She's wearing...(a BLOUSE) |
> | Picture 11? | 11. She's wearing...(a SKIRT) |
> | Picture 12? | 12. She's wearing...(a DRESS) |
> | Picture 13? | 13. She's wearing...(a SCARF) |
> | Picture 14? | 14. She's wearing...(SHOES) |
> | Picture 15? | 15. She's wearing...(a SWEATER) |
> | Picture 16? | 16. She's wearing...(a COAT) |

≡ B.2   Observe Colors.

Situation: Dave and Tom are talking about a party.

> Dave: What did Paul wear to the party last night?
> Tom: He wore a BLACK suit, a WHITE shirt, a BLUE and
>   ORANGE tie, dark BROWN shoes, and a GRAY
>   overcoat.
>
> Dave: What did his wife wear?
> Tom: She wore a GREEN dress, a YELLOW scarf, brown
>   high-heel shoes, and a RED coat.

Exercise 6.3   Practice Colors and Clothing.

Example: Teacher   Student

What are your wearing, Mr. A? I'm wearing a sport coat, a green
                                                 shirt, and dark blue slacks.

1. What are you wearing,   5. Are you wearing green socks?
     Mr. B?   6. Did you wear a white shirt yesterday?
2. Are you wearing a dress,   7. Did you wear orange shoes yesterday?
     Mr. C?   8. Did you wear yellow slacks yesterday?
3. Is he wearing a gray   9. What are you going to wear tomorrow?
     sport coat?   10. What is he going to wear tomorrow?
4. Are you wearing pajamas?

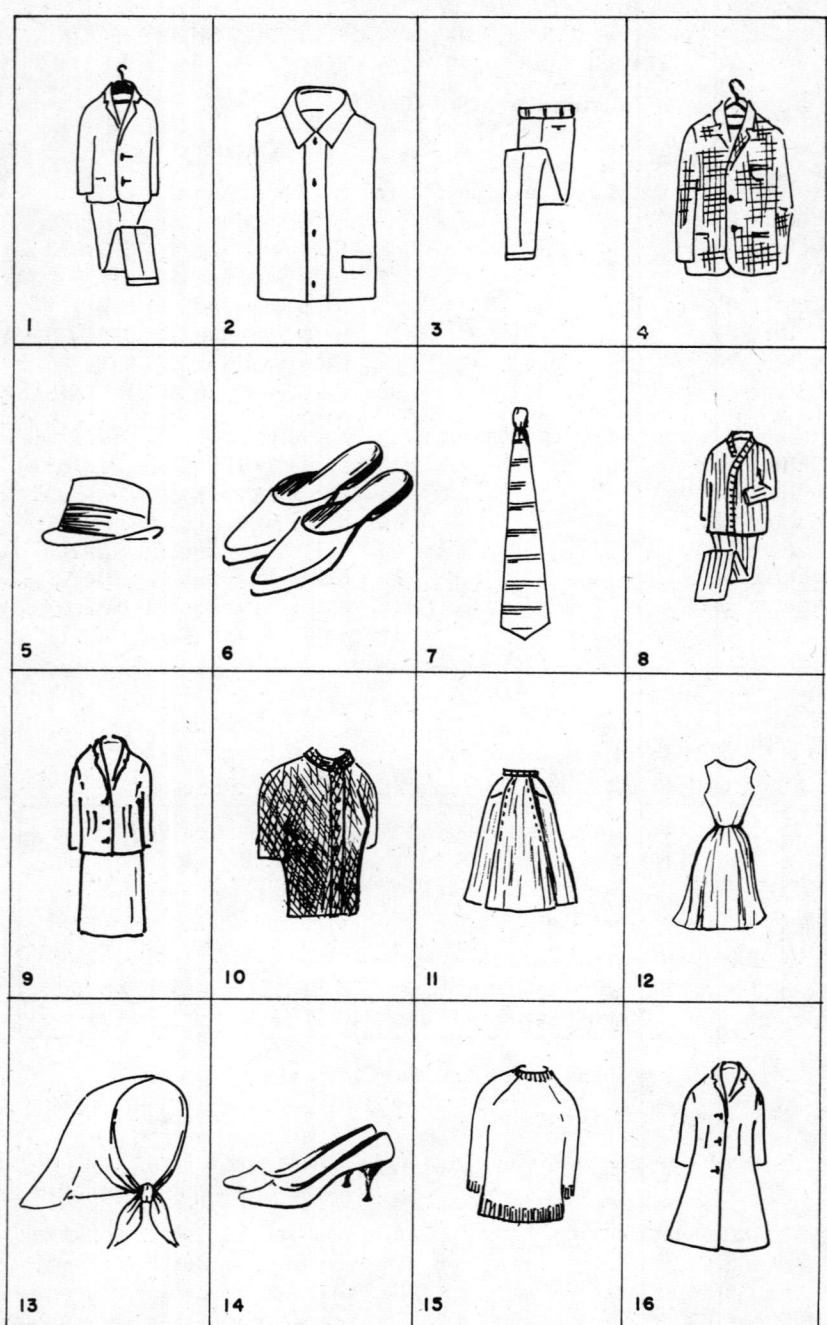

≡ C.   Observe Quantity and Number expressions.

> Situation: Marie and Susan live in an apartment. Marie bought some groceries.

Susan: Did you buy any fruit this morning?
Marie: Yes. I bought a FEW apples and A LOT OF cherries.

Susan: What else did you buy?
Marie: I bought A LITTLE meat and A LOT OF rice.

Susan: What about bread, potatoes, and cookies?
Marie: I didN'T buy MUCH bread or MANY potatoes, but
      I bought SEVERAL kinds of cookies.

Susan: HOW MUCH money did you spend?
Marie: NOT MUCH. Seven dollars and seventeen cents.

Exercise 6.4   Practice A FEW, A LITTLE, etc.

Examples: Teacher   Student

Did Marie buy a lot of apples?   No, she bought a few apples.
Did she buy a lot of bread?   No, she didn't buy much bread.

1. Did she buy a lot of meat?   6. How much meat and how many
2. Did she buy a few cherries?   apples did she buy?
3. Did she buy a little rice?   7. How much rice and how many
4. Did she buy a lot of potatoes?   cherries did she buy?
5. Did she buy one kind of   8. How much bread and how
    cookies?   many potatoes did she buy?

≡ D.   Observe MISS, LOSE, WASTE.

> Situation: Dave is writing a letter.

This morning I woke up late and MISSED breakfast. I also
missed my bus and my first class. During my second
class I missed several examination questions. My
grade was 60.

This afternoon I LOST my pen. I bought a new, inexpensive one, but it wasn't very good.

It was a very bad day. I WASTED my time this morning
and I wasted my money this afternoon.

Exercise 6.5   Practice MISS, LOSE, WASTE.

Examples: Teacher   Student

    Which class did Dave miss?   He missed his first class.
    How did he waste his money?   He bought a cheap pen.

1. What did Dave lose?
2. What did Dave miss?
3. What did he waste?
4. How did Dave waste his
   money?
5. Did you lose your book
   yesterday?

6. What did you lose yesterday?
7. Did your friend lose his coat
   yesterday?
8. Do you sometimes miss breakfast?
9. Do your friends ever miss dinner?
10. How many questions are you going to
    miss on the next examination?

E.   Observe Distance and Time expressions.

Situation: Don is asking Bob about his trip to Chicago.

> Don: HOW FAR did you drive Saturday?
> Bob: I drove AS FAR AS Chicago. It's about TWO HUN-
>   DRED AND FIFTY MILES from here.
>
> Don: HOW LONG did you drive?
> Bob: SIX HOURS. I left at three and drove UNTIL nine.

NOTE: AS FAR AS indicates distance; UNTIL indicates
       time.

Exercise 6.6   Practice AS FAR AS and UNTIL.

Examples: Teacher   Student

    How far did Bob drive?   He drove as far as Chicago.
    How long did he drive?   He drove until nine o'clock.

1. How far did Bob go?
2. How far do you walk every
   noon?
3. How far did you drive last
   weekend?
4. How long did you drive?
5. How long do you study every
   night?

6. How far did you walk last Saturday?
7. How long did you watch TV last
   night?
8. How far are you going to walk next
   Sunday?
9. How long are you going to study
   tomorrow night?
10. How long are you going to be here?

Summary Dialogue.

    Situation: Mr. and Mrs. Brown are shopping. It's Friday night.

Mr. Brown:	How late is it?
Mrs. Brown:	It's eight thirty. The stores close in half an hour.

Mr. Brown:	Did you finish your shopping?
Mrs. Brown:	No, I only found a few things.

Mr. Brown:	What did you buy?
Mrs. Brown:	I bought a nail file, a few needles, two spools of thread, and a pair of shoes.

Mr. Brown:	I looked at the typewriters, the cameras, and the record players. They're all very expensive.

Mrs. Brown:	Shall we go?
Mr. Brown:	No, let's have a cup of coffee first.

Mrs. Brown:	How long will it take?
Mr. Brown:	Only a few minutes.
Mrs. Brown:	All right.

Homework.

Write a short conversation. Use: Clothing and Colors, Parts and Functions of the body, Quantity and Distance expressions, and the verbs MISS and LOSE.

Lesson VII

A. MAKE, DO.
B. Daily Activities.
C. Family Relationships.
D. A Home, Rooms, Furniture.

Review Dialogue.

Situation: John and Bill are talking about a party.

John: What are you going to wear Friday night?
Bill: I'm going to wear my dark suit, a white shirt, a light blue tie, and, of course, black shoes and socks.

John: Who are you taking?
Bill: A very beautiful girl. She has long blonde hair, blue eyes, fair skin, rosy cheeks, a small nose, a wonderful smile, and a very good figure.

John: Is her name Mary?
Bill: Yes, it is. Do you know her?
John: Yes. She's my sister's best friend.

≡ A. Observe MAKE and DO.

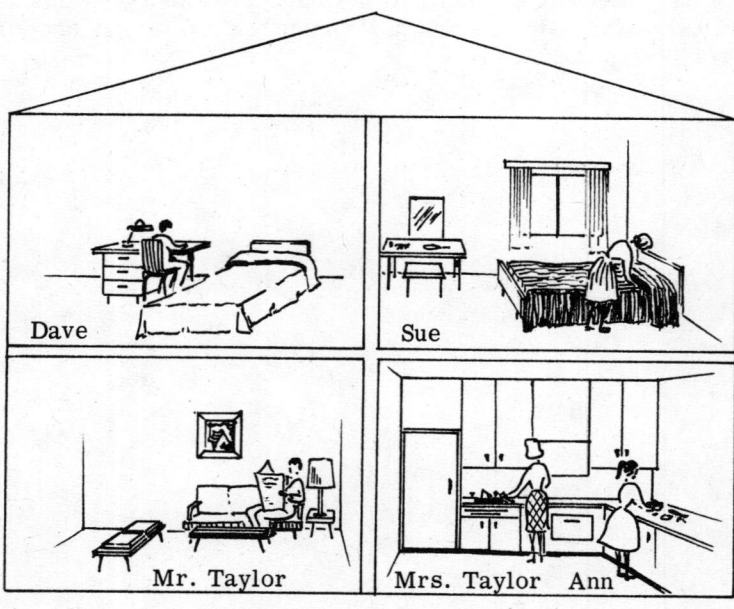

44

(Please look at the picture.)

Situation: It's about five forty-five in the afternoon.

Mr. Taylor is in the living room. He's reading the evening paper. He works in a factory.

He MAKES a lot of MONEY. Last year he earned about $10,000.

After dinner Mr. Taylor is going to MAKE a plane RESERVATION for Saturday morning. He's going to MAKE a SPEECH in Chicago Saturday night.

Mrs. Taylor and her daughter, Ann, are in the kitchen. They are preparing dinner. Ann is DOING a FAVOR for her mother. She's MAKING a SALAD.

Mrs. Taylor MADE a PIE for dessert. Now she's washing some of the dishes. She and Ann will DO the other DISHES after dinner.

Dave is in his bedroom. He's DOING his HOMEWORK carefully. He MADE a lot of MISTAKES yesterday. He's MAKING very slow PROGRESS in English. Tomorrow he's going to MAKE an APPOINT-MENT with his teacher.

Sue is in her bedroom. She's MAKING her BED. She MADE a DRESS this afternoon. Her boyfriend MADE a DATE with her for Friday night.

NOTE: Use DO with A FAVOR, THE DISHES, HOMEWORK.

Exercise 7.1   Practice MAKE.

Example: <u>Teacher</u>   <u>Student</u>

What does Mr. Taylor make?   He makes a lot of money.

1. What kind of reservation is he going to make?
2. What is he going to do in Chicago?
3. What is Ann making in the kitchen?
4. What did her mother make?
5. How many mistakes did Dave make yesterday?
6. Is he making good progress?
7. Is he going to make a date with his teacher?
8. Is Sue making Dave's bed?
9. What did she make this afternoon?
10. Did her boyfriend make an appointment with her?

Exercise 7.2   Practice DO.

Example: <u>Teacher</u>   <u>Student</u>

 Who was doing his homework? Dave was doing his homework.

1. Was Sue doing a favor for her
   mother?
2. Who will do the dishes after
   dinner?
3. Mr. A, do you ever do the dishes?
4. Mr. B, when do you usually do
   your homework?
5. Who do you sometimes do
   favors for?
6. When do you do your laundry?

Exercise 7.3   Practice DO and MAKE.

Examples: <u>Teacher</u>   <u>Student</u>

 a lot of money yesterday He made a lot of money yesterday.
 the work badly this morning He did the work badly this morning.

1. $12,000 last year
2. the homework yesterday
   afternoon
3. the coffee this morning
4. the dishes last night
5. a cake yesterday
6. a sandwich this noon
7. Lesson 4 last Monday
8. a train reservation
9. a lot of progress in Philosophy
10. an appointment with the dentist
11. several bad mistakes
12. a date with the secretary
13. a favor for the nurse
14. a speech about factories

≡ B.1   Observe Daily Activities.

 Situation: Mr. Green is having lunch with his son Edward.

Mr. Green:	What did you do this morning, son?
Edward:	Lots of things, Dad. I WOKE UP at seven, GOT UP at seven ten, TOOK A SHOWER, SHAVED, BRUSHED my TEETH, DRESSED, and WENT to breakfast.
	After breakfast I LEFT the dormitory and RAN to class. I was two minutes late. The teacher asked me, ''Why are you late?'' I explained, ''My watch STOPPED this morning.'' It stopped at seven fifteen. I HAD classes all morning.
Mr. Green:	You certainly didn't waste any time. Please pass me the salt. Now tell me what you are going to do this afternoon.
Edward:	Here's the salt. I'll GO to another class at two, WORK at the bookstore from three to five, REST for an hour, and HAVE dinner. Tonight I'm going to a basketball game with some friends.

Exercise 7.4   Practice Daily Activities.

Examples: <u>Teacher</u>   <u>Student</u>

What time did Edward wake up?   He woke up at seven.
Did he get up at seven?   No, he got up at seven ten.

1. What did he do before breakfast?
2. What did he do after breakfast?
3. Why was he late to class?
4. How long did he have classes?
5. Does he have any classes this afternoon?
6. What is he going to do after that class?
7. Where is he going tonight?

8. Mr. A, what did you do this morning?
9. What are you going to do this afternoon?
10. What did you do last night?
11. What are you going to do this evening?

≡ B.2   Observe these Evening Activities.

Jim: What do you do before a date?
Tom: I always POLISH my shoes with SHOE POLISH,
              SHAVE with my ELECTRIC RAZOR,
              WASH my hands, face, neck, and ears with SOAP,
              RINSE them with WATER,
              DRY them with a TOWEL, and
              BRUSH my hair with a HAIRBRUSH.

Jim: Do you ever COMB your hair?
Tom: No. My hair is too short.

Exercise 7.5   Practice some Evening Activities.

Examples: <u>Teacher</u>   <u>Student</u>

What do you comb your hair with?   I use a comb.
What do you polish your shoes with?   I use shoe polish.

1. What do you wash with?
2. Do you rinse with a towel?
3. What do you dry your ears with?
4. Do you brush your hair with a shoe brush?
5. What do you shave with?
6. Do you use an electric razor or a safety razor?

7. What do you brush your teeth with?
8. What do women polish their nails with?
9. What do people brush their clothes with?
10. What do girls file their nails with?

☰ C. Observe Family Relationships.[1]

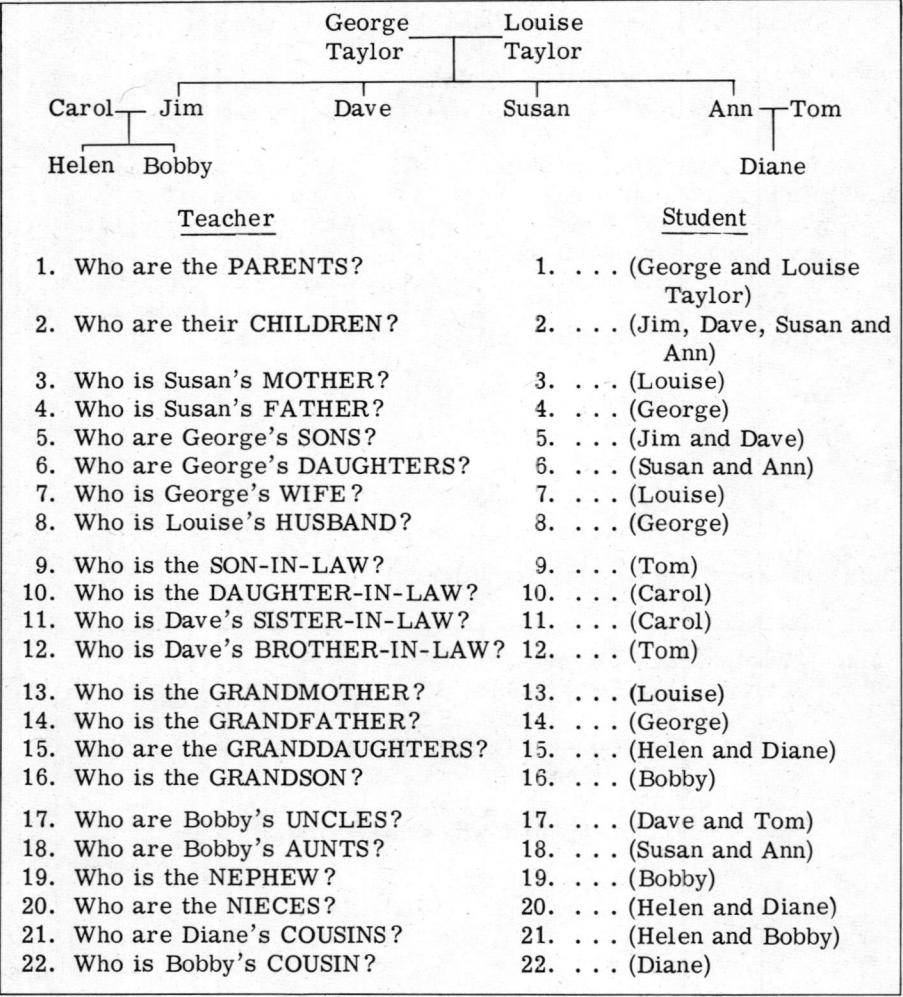

Teacher	Student
1. Who are the PARENTS?	1. . . . (George and Louise Taylor)
2. Who are their CHILDREN?	2. . . . (Jim, Dave, Susan and Ann)
3. Who is Susan's MOTHER?	3. . . . (Louise)
4. Who is Susan's FATHER?	4. . . . (George)
5. Who are George's SONS?	5. . . . (Jim and Dave)
6. Who are George's DAUGHTERS?	6. . . . (Susan and Ann)
7. Who is George's WIFE?	7. . . . (Louise)
8. Who is Louise's HUSBAND?	8. . . . (George)
9. Who is the SON-IN-LAW?	9. . . . (Tom)
10. Who is the DAUGHTER-IN-LAW?	10. . . . (Carol)
11. Who is Dave's SISTER-IN-LAW?	11. . . . (Carol)
12. Who is Dave's BROTHER-IN-LAW?	12. . . . (Tom)
13. Who is the GRANDMOTHER?	13. . . . (Louise)
14. Who is the GRANDFATHER?	14. . . . (George)
15. Who are the GRANDDAUGHTERS?	15. . . . (Helen and Diane)
16. Who is the GRANDSON?	16. . . . (Bobby)
17. Who are Bobby's UNCLES?	17. . . . (Dave and Tom)
18. Who are Bobby's AUNTS?	18. . . . (Susan and Ann)
19. Who is the NEPHEW?	19. . . . (Bobby)
20. Who are the NIECES?	20. . . . (Helen and Diane)
21. Who are Diane's COUSINS?	21. . . . (Helen and Bobby)
22. Who is Bobby's COUSIN?	22. . . . (Diane)

Exercise 7.6   Practice Family Relationships.

Examples: Teacher	Student
Who are your parents' children?	My brothers and sisters.
Who are your grandfathers?	My mother's father and my father's father.

1. Who are your uncles?
2. Who are your aunts?
3. Who are your nieces?
4. Who are your nephews?
5. Who are your cousins?
6. Is your father's brother your aunt?
7. Is your mother's father your uncle?
8. Is your brother's wife your aunt?
9. Is your brother's son your niece?
10. Is your grandfather's daughter your sister?

NOTE TO TEACHER: [1]Put diagram on blackboard.

☰ D.1   Observe HOUSE, GARAGE, etc.

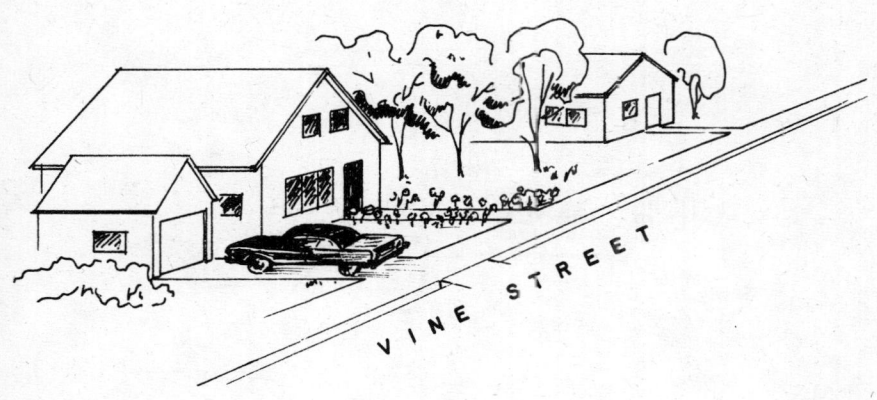

Teacher	Student
What's beside the house?	. . . (The GARAGE) is beside the house.
1. What's in front of the garage?	1. . . . (The CAR) is in front of the garage.
2. Where's the car?	2. It's in . . . (the DRIVEWAY).
3. What's on both sides of the driveway?	3. . . . (The LAWN) is on both sides of the driveway.
4. What's between the lawn and the street?	4. . . . (The SIDEWALK) is between the lawn and the street).
5. What's between the sidewalk and the house?	5. . . . (The front WALK) is between the sidewalk and the house.
6. What's AROUND the house?	6. . . . (The YARD) is around the house.
7. Where are the trees?	7. They're . . . (in the yard).
8. Where are the BUSHES?	8. They're . . . (NEXT TO the garage).
9. Where are the FLOWERS?	9. They're . . . (beside the walk).
10. Where do the NEIGHBORS live?	10. They live . . . (in the other house).

≡ D.2   Observe Rooms and Furniture.

a.

Teacher	Student
Which room is this?	It's . . . (the LIVING ROOM)
1. Where's the arm chair?	1. It's . . . (near the TELEVISION)
2. Where's the TELEVISION?	2. It's between . . . (the arm chair and the FIREPLACE)
3. Where's the fireplace?	3. It's between . . . (the CURTAINS)
4. Where are the curtains?	4. They're . . . (on the WALL)
5. What are some of the curtains near?	5. They're near . . . (the FLOOR LAMP)
6. Where's the floor lamp?	6. It's beside . . . (the SOFA)[1]
7. Where's the sofa?	7. It's in back of . . . (the COFFEE TABLE)
8. Where's the sofa?	8. It's beside . . . (the END TABLE)
9. Where's the sofa?	9. It's between . . . (the floor lamp and the TABLE LAMP)
10. What's the table lamp on?	10. It's on . . . (the end table)
11. Where are the CUSHIONS?	11. They're . . . (on the sofa)
12. Where's the ASHTRAY?	12. It's . . . (on the coffee table)
13. Where's the rug?[1]	13. It's . . . (under the coffee table, the arm chair, and the TV)
14. Where's the MAGAZINE RACK?	14. It's . . . (beside the arm chair)

NOTE TO TEACHER: [1]Additional items: couch, davenport, carpet.

b.

Teacher	Student
Which room is this?	It's . . . (the BEDROOM)
1. Where's the DRESSER?	1. It's beside . . . (the BED)
2. Where's the bed?	2. It's between . . . (the dresser and the chair)
3. Where's the chair?	3. It's . . . (at the desk)
4. What's the desk near?	4. It's near . . . (the BOOKCASE)
5. What's the bookcase near?	5. It's near . . . (the CLOSET)
6. Where's the closet?	6. It's . . . (in the wall)
7. Where're the clothes and the shoes?	7. They're . . . (in the closet)
8. Where're the books?	8. They're . . . (in the bookcase)
9. Where're the flowers?	9. They're . . . (on the bookcase)
10. Where're the PILLOWS and the BLANKETS?	10. They're . . . (on the bed)
11. Where's the BEDSPREAD?	11. It's . . . (ON TOP OF the pillows and blankets)
12. Where're the SHEETS?	12. They're . . . (under the blankets)

c.

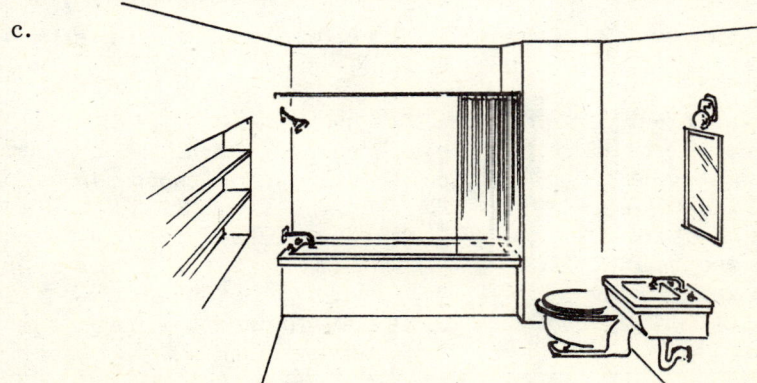

Teacher	Student
Which room is this?	It's . . . (the BATHROOM)

1. Where's the MIRROR?	1. It's above . . . (the WASH BASIN)
2. Where's the wash basin?	2. It's beside . . . (the TOILET)
3. What's the toilet near?	3. It's near . . . (the BATHTUB)
4. Where's the SHOWER?	4. It's . . . (above the bathtub)
5. What kind of curtains are those?	5. They're . . . (SHOWER CURTAINS)
6. Where's the MEDICINE CABINET?	6. It's . . . (in back of the mirror)
7. Where are the FAUCETS?	7. They're . . . (on the wash basin)
8. Which is the hot water faucet?	8. . . . (the left one)
9. Where's the LIGHT?	9. It's . . . (above the mirror)

d.

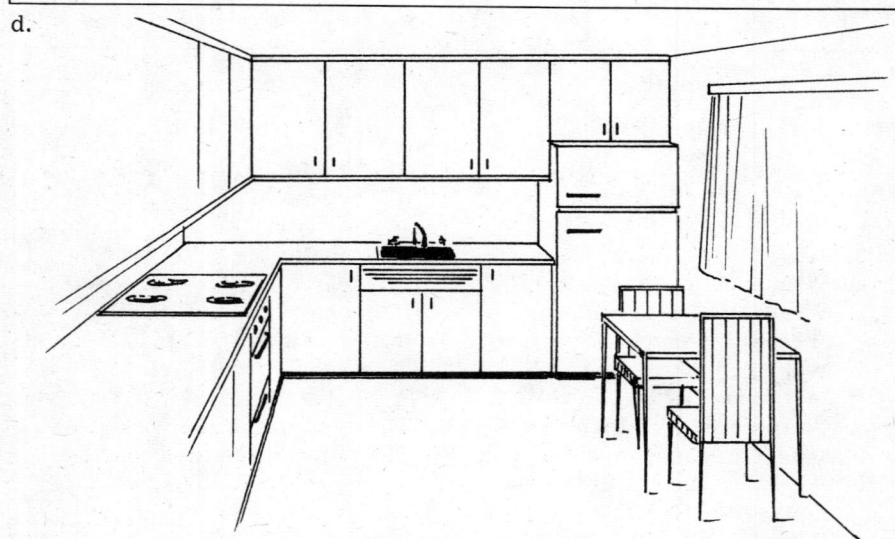

Teacher	Student
Which room is this?	It's . . . (the KITCHEN)
1. Where's the table?	1. It's between . . . (the chairs)
2. What're the table and chairs near?	2. They're near . . . (the REFRIGERATOR)[1]
3. Where's the refrigerator?	3. It's below . . . (a CUPBOARD)
4. What's the refrigerator near?	4. It's near . . . (the SINK)
5. Where's the sink?	5. It's above . . . (a cupboard)
6. What's the sink near?	6. It's near . . . (the STOVE)
7. Where is the OVEN?	7. It's . . . (in the stove)
8. Where are the BURNERS?[2]	8. They're . . . (on top of the stove)
9. Where are the faucets?	9. They're . . . (on the sink)
10. Where is the FREEZER?	10. It's . . . (in the top of the refrigerator)

NOTES TO TEACHER: [1] You will also hear ICEBOX.
[2] Gas stoves have BURNERS; electric stoves have HEATING ELEMENTS.

Exercise 7.7   Practice the Rooms of a House.

Example: Teacher   Student

Do people sleep in the closet?   No, they sleep in the bedroom.

1. Do people take showers in the kitchen?
2. Do people sleep in the bathroom?
3. Do people do the dishes in the living room?
4. Do people watch TV in the bathroom?
5. Do people dress in the yard?
6. Do people prepare food in the bedroom?
7. Do people brush their teeth in the garage?
8. Do people plant flowers in the bedroom?
9. Do people park their cars in the clothes closet?
10. Do people wash their cars in the living room?

Summary Dialogue.

Professor White's Art class is studying dishes. They are going to visit a dish factory this afternoon. Professor White told everyone, "Let's meet at the factory at one o'clock. Please don't be late. I made our appointment with the manager for one fifteen."

Robert made a date with Barbara for the afternoon. She lives with several other girls. She usually eats lunch last and always does the lunch dishes. Robert rode his bicycle to her house, parked it in the yard, and is in the house now.

Robert: Hurry up, Barbara, or we'll miss the streetcar.
Barbara: Didn't you bring your car?
Robert: No. My roommate is using it. Hurry up!
Barbara: I am hurrying. Stop saying that, or you'll make me mad.

They arrived at the factory on time and followed the others around the factory. After the tour, Robert said, "They make very nice dishes. Shall I buy you some?"

Barbara said, "No, thank you. I do enough dishes already."

Homework.

Write a short story. Use: MAKE and DO, parts of a House, Family Relationships, and Daily Activities.

Lesson VIII

A. Introductions.
B. Irregular Past Forms of Verbs.
C. LOOK AT, LISTEN TO, etc; ENTER, ATTEND, etc.
D. SPEAK, TALK, SAY, TELL.
E. -ION, -TION, -ATION: DISCUSSION, LOCATION, EXAMINATION, etc.

Review Dialogue.

Father: What did you do this morning, son?
Son: First, I backed the car out of the garage, parked it in the
        driveway, and washed it. Then, I mowed the lawn and
        cut some flowers.

Father: Did you make anything?
Son: Yes, I did. I made another bulletin board.

Father: How many bulletin boards do we have now?
Son: Five. You bought two and I made the others.

A. Observe the following Introduction.[1]

Situation: Jerry meets his old friend Bill and introduces him to
           his family.

Jerry: Bill, it's good to see you. How've you been?
Bill: Fine, Jerry. You're looking good.
Jerry: Thanks, I never change. Do you have a few minutes?
        I'd like you to meet my family.
Bill: Yes, of course.

Jerry: This is my wife Kay, my son Billy, and my daughter
        Caroline. And this is Bill Jones.
Bill: I'm very pleased to meet you.

(The children say, "Hello.")
Kay: We're happy to meet you, Bill. Jerry often talks
        about you.
Bill: We were very close friends during our school days.

Jerry: Here comes my cousin Joyce. I think you met her
        several years ago.
Bill: Do you mean your skinny little cousin? She certainly
        has changed.

NOTE TO TEACHER: [1]See Lesson 1, page 7 for a few other expressions.

Exercise 8.1   Practice Introductions.

    a. I'd like you to meet my family.
                      . . . my father
                      . . . my sister
                      . . . my brother
                      . . . my wife
                      . . . my roommate

    b. Jerry introduced Bill to his family.
                   . . . him . . his father
                   . . . him . . his sister
            . . . his friend . . his teacher
            . . . his friend . . his girlfriend
        . . . his girlfriend . . his parents

c. <u>Teacher</u>	<u>Student</u>
1. Do you introduce old men to young men?[1]	1. . . . (No, you introduce young men to old men.)
2. Do you introduce women to men?	2. . . . (No, you introduce men to women.)
3. Do you introduce your teacher to your friend?	3. . . . (No, you introduce your friend to your teacher.)
4. Do men shake hands in the United States?	4. . . . (Yes, they do.)
5. When do men shake hands with women?	5. . . . (When the woman offers her hand.)
6. Do people bow in the United States?	6. . . . (No, they don't.)

NOTE TO TEACHER: [1]The nonpersonal use of YOU.

≡ B.1 Observe the Irregular Past Forms.

Situation: Paul meets Jack at a restaurant.

Paul: Hi, Jack. I SAW you with a pretty
      girl at the movies last Saturday

Jack: Yes, I was there. I HAD a terrible
      experience.

Paul: What happened?

Jack: Saturday afternoon I MET a nice girl.
      Her name was Barbara. We CAME
      to this restaurant, SAT DOWN and
      BEGAN to talk. We DRANK
      coffee and talked for two hours.
      I invited her to the movies and
      she SAID, "Thank you."

      I WENT home and WROTE some
      letters. Then I TOOK a shower,
      changed my clothes and ATE
      dinner. I LEFT home at seven
      and MET Barbara. We walked to
      the theater. I GOT in the line for
      a ticket. At the ticket window I
      reached for my wallet, but I
      couldn't find it. My face BECAME
      red and I was very embarrassed.
      I said, "Barbara, I'm sorry. I
      FORGOT my wallet."

Past	Simple
SAW	SEE
HAD	HAVE
MET	MEET
CAME	COME
SAT	SIT
BEGAN	BEGIN
DRANK	DRINK
SAID	SAY
WENT	GO
WROTE	WRITE
TOOK	TAKE
ATE	EAT
LEFT	LEAVE
GOT	GET
BECAME	BECOME
TOLD	TELL
FORGOT	FORGET
LENT	LEND
BOUGHT	BUY

Paul: Did you borrow some money from her?

Jack: Yes. She LENT me two dollars and I BOUGHT the tickets.

Exercise 8.2   Practice the past forms of SEE, HAVE, MEET, etc.

Examples: <u>Teacher</u>   <u>Student</u>

Where did Paul see Jack last   He saw Jack at the movies.
   Saturday?

Was Jack with his roommate?   No, he was with a pretty girl.

1. Did Jack have a good experience
    at the movies?
2. Who did Jack meet Saturday
    afternoon?
3. What did they do at the res-
    taurant?
4. Did they begin to sing?
5. Did they drink milk?
6. Did Barbara say, "No, thank
    you. I'm busy."?
7. Where did Jack go then?
8. What did he write?

9. Did he take a bath?
10. Did he eat lunch?
11. When did he leave home?
12. Did Barbara get in the line at
     the theater?
13. What did Jack forget?
14. What color did his face become?
15. What did he say to Barbara?
16. What did Jack borrow from
     Barbara?
17. How much money did Barbara
     lend him?
18. What did he buy with the money?

Exercise 8.3 Practice BORROW and LEND.

a. May I borrow your pen?
               your book
               your pencil
               your car

b. Can you lend me a pencil?
                 a piece of paper
                 a dime
                 a quarter
                 five dollars

c. 1. How much money did Jack borrow? (He borrowed two dollars.)
    2. What did I borrow from you?
    3. Did I borrow a pen from you?
    4. What did you borrow from your roommate yesterday?
    5. What would you like to borrow from him?
    6. How much money did Barbara lend Jack?
    7. What did you lend me?
    8. Did you lend me a dime?
    9. What did your roommate lend you yesterday?
   10. What do you want him to lend you?

≡ B.2 Observe the Irregular Past Forms.

Situation: Chuck receives a letter from his little sister,
              Betty. Jimmy is their baby brother. He's four
              years old.

Dear Brother,

I SENT you a letter last week. Why didn't you answer it? Are you sick? I FELT sick last Tuesday but I'm well now.

I FOUND some of your books in the basement. Mother said that you GAVE them to me last year. I CHOSE two of them, and Mother and I TOOK them to the bookstore. I SOLD them for five dollars and BOUGHT a new book. It COST me five dollars and twenty cents. I READ part of my new book last night. It's an adventure story and it's very exciting.

Jimmy was a bad boy yesterday. He TOOK one of Mother's dishes outside. He was playing with it and FELL down. He dropped the dish and it BROKE into little pieces. He also TORE his pants. He BROUGHT the broken pieces in the house and PUT them on the kitchen table. Mother spanked him and SENT him to bed.

Please write soon.

                            Betty

Exercise 8.4   Practice the past forms of SEND, FEEL, etc.

Examples: <u>Teacher</u>   <u>Student</u>

Who did Betty send a letter to?   She sent a letter to her brother.
Did Betty's brother feel sick
      last Tuesday?   No, Betty felt sick.

1. What did Betty find in the
      basement?
2. Did her mother give them to her?
3. How many books did she choose?
4. Where did she and her mother
      take the books?
5. Did Betty sell each book for
      five dollars?
6. How many new books did she buy?
7. How much did the new book cost?

8. Did she read the entire book?
9. Did Betty fall down?
10. What did Jimmy break?
11. What did he tear?
12. What did he do with the
      broken dish?
13. Did he put the pieces on the
      coffee table?
14. Where did Jimmy's mother
      send him?

☰ C.   Observe Verbs With Prepositions and Without Prepositions.

Situation: A young boy is writing a story for his teacher.

My sister and I went to the park last weekend. We saw
many very interesting things.

We arrived at the park at nine o'clock in the morning.
First we went to the Garden and LOOKED AT the flowers. They
were very beautiful and smelled very nice. Then we went to the
Aviary and LISTENED TO the birds. They sang very beautifully.
Then we saw the seals. They did funny tricks and we LAUGHED
AT them a lot.

After lunch we ENTERED the Zoo. We WATCHED the
monkeys for a long time. We looked at some of the other
animals too but we didn't watch them. They were all taking
their afternoon naps. Then we ATTENDED a puppet show. We
left the park at four-thirty and went home.

We ENJOYED our visit to the park very much.

NOTES: The verbs with prepositions are LOOK AT, LISTEN TO,
          LAUGH AT.
       The verbs without prepositions are: ENTER, WATCH,
          ATTEND, ENJOY.

Exercise 8.5   Practice LOOK AT, etc.; ENTER, etc.

a. Example: <u>Teacher</u>   <u>Student</u>

      Where did the boy and his sister   They went to the park.
         go last weekend?

1. What did they do first?
2. What did they do in the Aviary?
3. Did they listen to the seals?
4. What did they do after lunch?
5. Did they look at the monkeys?

6. Did they watch the other animals?
7. What did they do after that?
8. Did they like their visit to to the park?

b. Example: <u>Teacher</u>   <u>Student</u>

            the park . . . went   They went to the park.

1. the Zoo . . . enter
2. the flowers . . . look
3. the puppet show . . . attend
4. the seals . . . laugh
5. the monkeys . . . watch

6. the birds . . . listen
7. their visit . . . enjoy
8. the other animals . . . look
9. home . . . go
10. the living room . . . enter

≡ D. Observe SPEAK, TALK; SAY,[1] TELL.

>   Professor Reed SPOKE to his class about winter this morning. It's noon now. Henry and his American roommate James are TALKING about the lecture.
>
> James: What did Professor Reed talk about this morning?
> Henry: Winter. He SAID, "I slept on the ice several times
>   last year."
> James: Are you sure he said, "I slept on the ice?"
>
> Henry: Yes. I heard it very clearly. He TOLD us several
>   stories. One time he broke his arm.
> James: I don't think you understood him correctly.
>
> Henry: Yes, I did. He slept on the ice and broke his arm.
> James: That's impossible. He meant, "I <u>slipped</u> on the ice
>   and broke my arm."

NOTES: SPEAK often indicates formality; TALK indicates an
          informal conversation.
         Use SAY with quotations; use TELL with STORY, etc.

NOTE TO TEACHER: [1]SAY TO and SAY THAT are in later lessons.

Exercise 8.6 Practice SPEAK, TALK, SAY, TELL.

a. 1. Who did Professor Reed speak to?
   2. Who did Henry talk to?
   3. What did Professor Reed say?
   4. What did he tell his class?

b. Professor Reed spoke to his class. c. Henry talked to his roommate.
   . . . to the students   . . . to his classmate.
   Dr. Brown . . .   . . . his friend.
   The professor . . .   . . . his brother.
   The director . . .   . . . his father.
   The president . . .   . . . his teacher.

d. Examples: Teacher   Student

   them a story   He told them a story.
   "I slipped on the ice"   He said, "I slipped on the ice."

   1. her a story   6. "Good afternoon"
   2. him a story   7. us about a movie
   3. him about a lecture   8. "I'm happy to meet you"
   4. "Thank you"   9. them about his country
   5. "Excuse me"   10. me the time

≡ E. Observe -ION, -TION, -ATION.

> Mary: Did you DISCUSS last night's lecture in class today?
>
> Joe: Yes, we talked about it for an hour. It was a good
>   DISCUSSION.

Exercise 8.7   Practice -ION, -TION, -ATION.

   Examples: Teacher   Student

   His discussion of the problem   He discussed the problem.
   Our examination of the patient   We examined the patient.

a. 1. His description of his friend
   2. Our explanation of the words
   3. Their correction of the homework
   4. Your interruption of the teacher
   5. His introduction of his cousin
   6. Her completion of the work
   7. Our observation of the birds

b. 8. His invention of this machine
   9. John's operation of the machine
  10. Their possession of this money
  11. His prevention of the mistake
  12. My translation of the sentence
  13. Mary's appreciation of the music
  14. Henry's repetition of the question

Summary Dialogue.

Don:　Bob, could you lend me five dollars? I invited a girl to the
　　　　movies and I'm broke. I'll pay you back on Monday.
Bob:　I'm sorry, Don. I only have five and I have a date tonight.

Don:　Could you lend me two dollars? Enough to pay for the tickets?
Bob:　All right. Here's two dollars.

Don:　Thank you, Bob. You're a true friend.
Bob:　Don't forget to pay me back on Monday.
Don:　I won't.

Homework.

Write about one of your recent experiences. Use ENTER, SAY,
TELL, LEND and several of the other verbs in this lesson.

Lesson IX

A. GET, KNOW, MEET.
B. Words of Direction.
C. Directions; NORTH, EAST, SOUTH, WEST.
D. -LY: PROMPTLY.
E. -ER, -OR: WORKER, ACTOR.

Review Dialogue.

Situation: Edward is telling a story.

Yesterday, my friend George and I walked downtown. We met my music teacher, Mr. Brown.

I said, "Hello, Mr. Brown."
He answered, "Hello, Edward. How are you?"
"Fine, thank you," I said. "I'd like to introduce my friend George Blue. George, this is Mr. Brown, my music teacher."

Mr. Brown and George shook hands and said "How do you do." After a few minutes George said:

"I'm very happy to have met you, Mr. Brown."
"It was nice meeting you, George. Edward, please say hello to your mother and father for me."
"I will, Sir."

≡ A.1 Observe GET.

Situation: John meets his brother at the airport.

> John: Hello Pete, I'm sorry I'm late. When did you arrive?
> Pete: Hi, John. I GOT here at seven-thirty. We were a half-hour early.
>
> John: Did you GET your suitcases?
> Pete: No, I didn't pick them up. They're in the baggage room.
>
> John: I GOT your telegram yesterday. Why did you come home?
>
> Pete: I GOT homesick.

NOTE: GET means *arrive, obtain, receive, become*.

Exercise 9.1   Practice GET.

a. Examples: <u>Teacher</u>   <u>Student</u>

When did you get to Ann Arbor?   I got to Ann Arbor in June.
How did you get here?   I got here by plane.

1. What time do you get to   6. How will you get home?
   school every morning?   7. How does your father get to work?
2. What time do you usually   8. How did you get from the airport
   get home?   to town?
3. When did you get to class   9. How did you get from the train
   this morning?   station to the university?
4. When did you get to the   10. How did you get from the bus
   movies last night?   station to the dormitory?
5. What time did you get to bed?

b. What did you get at the store?   I got some groceries.
   Did you get a letter in the mail?   No, I got a package.

1. Where did you get your books?   6. Did you get some money from
2. Did you get your suit in Detroit?   home yesterday?
3. Where did you get your pen?   7. How many letters did you get
4. Are you going to get a car?   today?
5. What did you get at the post   8. Did you get a package from
   office?   home yesterday?

c. When did your friend get well?   He got well last weekend.
   Does it get cool in the afternoon?   No, it gets warm in the
                                           afternoon.

1. How many times did you get sick   7. Does the weather get hot
   last month?   during the night?
2. When do you always get tired?   8. Does it get cold in the after-
3. Did you get homesick during the   noon?
   course?   9. When does the weather get
4. Do you sometimes get sleepy   cool?
   after lunch?   10. When does it get warm?
5. When do you usually get hungry? 11. Are you getting old?
6. When do you often get thirsty?   12. When does it get dark?[1]

NOTE TO TEACHER: [1]For advanced classes: fat, bald, wet, better,
worse, jealous, ready, confused, discouraged, excited.

≡ A.2   Observe KNOW and MEET.

Situation: Harry and his uncle are at a picnic. Harry is a teenager.
His uncle is a little deaf.

Harry: Uncle Joe, do you KNOW that girl over there?
Uncle: What? What did you say? I don't hear very well, YOU KNOW.

Harry: Are you acquainted with that girl in the light blue dress?
Uncle: Who? Oh, her. Yes, of course, I know her. She's our
         neighbor's daughter. Why?

Harry: I'd like to MEET her. Will you introduce me to her?
Uncle: I DON'T KNOW, young fellow. She seldom likes boys with
         freckles and red hair.

Harry: Please don't say that, Uncle Joe.
Uncle: Very well, I'll introduce you. Let's walk over there.

NOTE: KNOW often means *be acquainted with.*
        MEET often means *be introduced to.*

Exercise 9.2   Practice KNOW and MEET.

a. Answer with a form of KNOW.

1. Why don't you talk to that man?   (I don't _____ him.)
2. Are you acquainted with Mrs. Blue   (Yes, I _____ her very well.)
3. Why didn't you introduce that man to   (She already _____ him.)
    your niece?
4. Is Mr. Jones a friend of yours?   (No, but he _____ my uncle.)
5. Is your cousin well-known here?   (Yes, everybody _____ him.)

b. Answer with a form of MEET.

1. Do you know Mr. Smith?   (Yes, I _____ him last night.)
2. Is my nephew Tom in your class?   (No, but I'd like to _____ him.)
3. Tom, do you know those people?   (Yes, I do. Would you like to
                                              _____ them?)
4. Does your sister know my wife?   (Yes, they _____ at the reception.)
5. Are you acquainted with my roommate?   (Yes, I _____ him yesterday.)

c. Answer with a form of KNOW or MEET.

1. Why don't you talk to that girl?
2. Do you know Miss Brown? (Yes . . . yesterday)
3. Are you acquainted with David? (Yes . . . very well)
4. Are you acquainted with Susan? (Yes . . . yesterday)
5. Is that girl in your class? (No, but . . .)
6. Why didn't you introduce your friend to your teacher?

☰ B. Observe words of Direction.

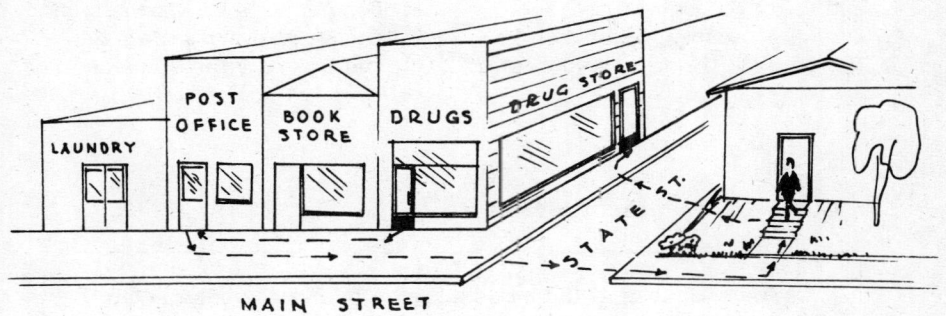

MAIN STREET

> Al needed some stamps so he went FROM his house TO the post office.
>
> He went OUT OF his house, DOWN the steps, THROUGH the yard, ACROSS State Street, INTO the drugstore and through it.
>
> He came out of the drugstore, walked PAST the bookstore, went into the post office, and got the stamps.
>
> After that he came out of the post office and walked ALONG Main Street. He went across State Street again, UP the steps and into his house.

NOTE: Use FROM, TO, DOWN, etc., with GO, WALK, COME, etc.

Exercise 9.3   Practice words of Direction.

Examples: <u>Teacher</u>   <u>Student</u>

Where did Al go?   He went from his house to
                                    the post office.

Did he go past the drugstore?   No, he went into it.

1. Did Al go out of his house and up the steps?
2. Did he go through the yard?
3. Did he go through State Street?
4. Did he go across the drugstore?
5. Did he walk through the bookstore?
6. Did he go into the bookstore?
7. Did he walk past the post office?
8. Did he go as far as the laundry?
9. Did he go across Main Street?
10. Did he go up the steps and out of his house?

≡ C.1   Observe Directions.   (Refer to picture on page 67.)

> Steve arrives at the bus station. He asks the bus driver, "Excuse me, HOW DO I GET to the post office?"
>
> The bus driver says, "I'm sorry, I don't know. Please ask inside."
>
> Steve goes inside the bus station and asks the ticket seller, "Excuse me, WHERE IS the post office?"
>
> The ticket seller says. "IT'S ON THE CORNER OF Central and Park."
>
> Steve asks, "How do I get there?"
>
> She says, "Go out the front door, turn RIGHT, walk STRAIGHT AHEAD, go to the corner, cross Central Avenue, turn LEFT, cross Main Street, and go one BLOCK. The post office is on the corner.
>
> Steve thanks the young lady, goes out the door, and turns in the wrong direction.

Exercise 9.4   Practice Directions.   (We are at the Bus Station.)

a.   Student A   Student B

Excuse me,
 . . . where is the post office?   It's on the corner of Central and
                                           Park.
         . . . the super market?   . . . on the other side of the Park.
         . . . the park?   . . . across the street.
         . . . the theater?   . . . next-door.
 . . . which way is the church?   . . . up Main Street.
         . . . the hotel?   . . . down Main Street.

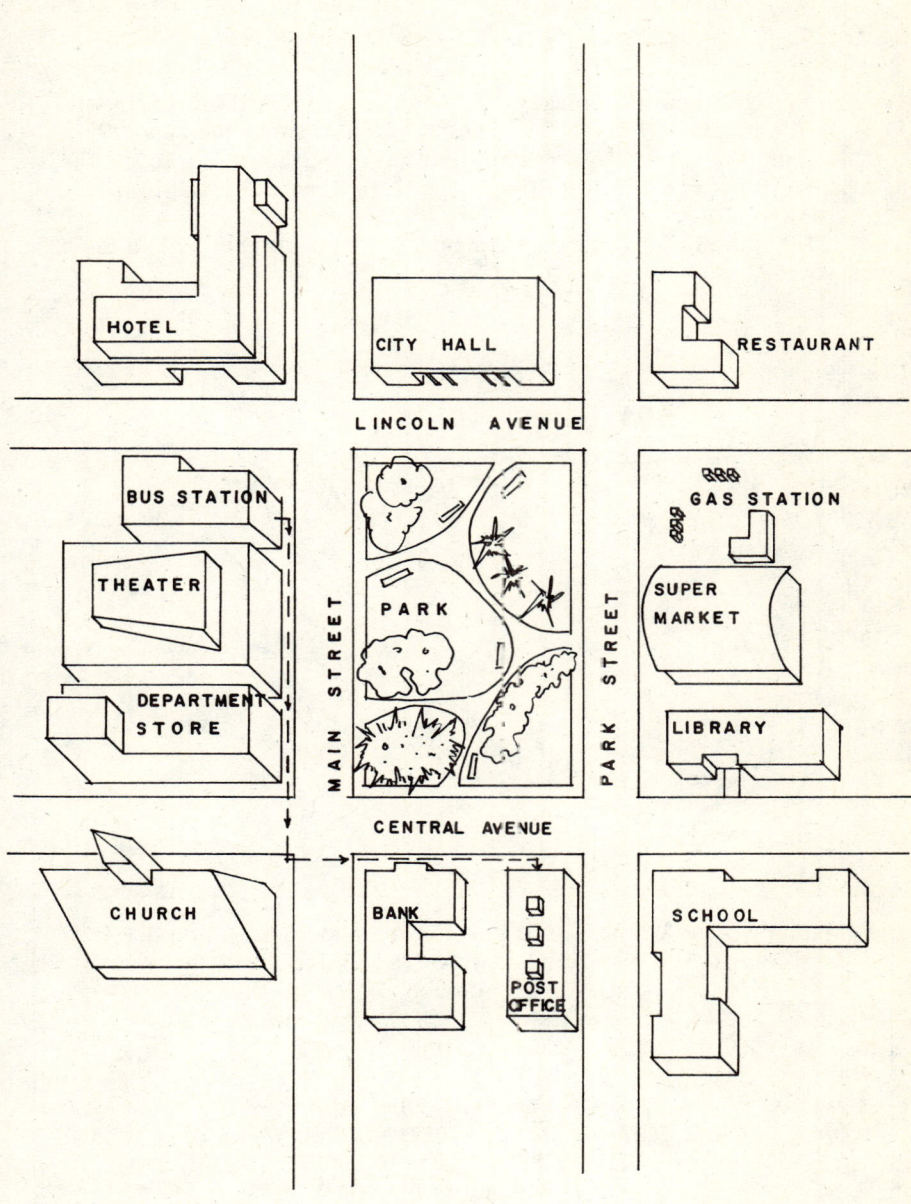

b. Example: <u>Teacher</u>   Student

     How do I get from the bus   Walk to the corner of Main and
       station to the library?   Central, turn left, cross Main
                                         Street, walk one block, and
                                         cross Park Street.

1. How do I get from the library   5. . . . from the department
   to the hotel?   store to the school?
2. . . . from the hotel to the restaurant? 6. from the school to the theater?
3. . . . from the restaurant to the   7. from the theater to the city
   bank?   hall?
4. . . . from the bank to the department   8. from the city hall to the
   store?   church?

≡C.2   Observe NORTH, EAST, SOUTH, WEST.

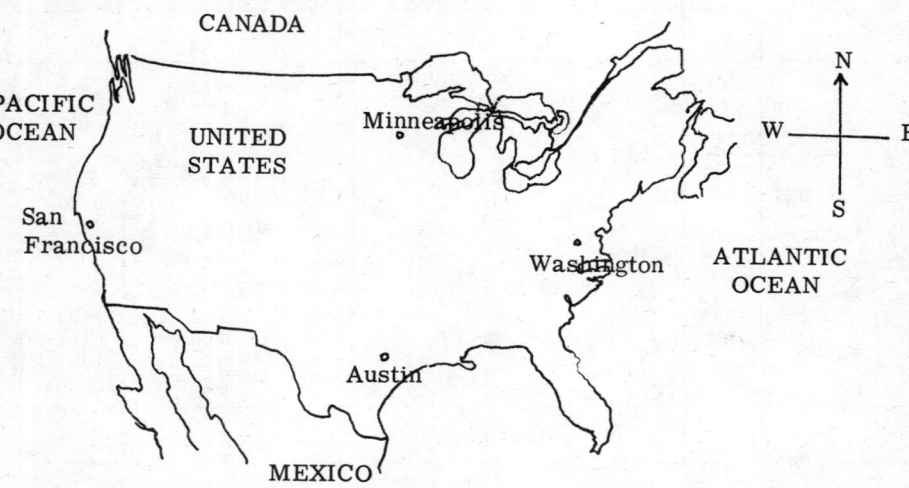

Marie:	Would you please tell me about the United States?
Mrs. Black:	Yes, with pleasure. The United States is NORTH OF Mexico, EAST OF the Pacific Ocean, SOUTH OF Canada, and WEST OF the Atlantic Ocean.
Marie:	What are some of the big cities?
Mrs. Black:	Minneapolis is in THE NORTH, Washington is in THE EAST, Austin is in THE SOUTH, and San Francisco is in THE WEST.
Marie:	Let me see. Minneapolis is A NORTHERN city, Washington is AN EASTERN city, Austin is A SOUTHERN city, and San Francisco is A WESTERN city.
Mrs. Black:	Yes, that's right.

Exercise 9.5   Practice NORTH, EAST, SOUTH, WEST.

Example: Teacher	Student
Is Canada north of the United States or south of the United States?	Canada is north of the United States.

1. Is the United States south of Mexico?
2. Which city is north of Austin?
3. Is the Atlantic Ocean east of the U. S. or west of the U. S.?
4. Is San Francisco east of Washington?
5. Which city is east of Minneapolis?
6. Is Washington in the North or in the East?
7. Where is Austin?
8. Is San Francisco in the North?
9. Which city is in the North?
10. Is Minneapolis a western city?
11. Is Austin a northern city?
12. Is Washington an eastern city or a western city?
13. What kind of city is San Francisco?

≡ D. Observe -LY.

> Mrs. Price invited several people to an afternoon tea. She wrote:
>
> > You are cordially invited to
> > an afternoon tea.
> > R.S.V.P.*
>
> Mr. Tower received one of the invitations. He was a handsome young man with dark brown hair. He telephoned Mrs. Price and said, "Thank you VERY MUCH for your invitation. I'll be there at four o'clock sharp."
>
> But, of course, Mr. Tower was late. After lunch that day he sat down in a chair and read a magazine. His eyes closed SLOWLY and he went to sleep. He woke up at four o'clock, dressed RAPIDLY, and hurried to Mrs. Price's house. She was waiting PATIENTLY.
>
> He said to his hostess in a very polite and sincere manner, "I'm very sorry that I'm late, Mrs. Price." She answered him very FORMALLY and CORRECTLY, "I'm happy that you were able to come, Mr. Tower." She poured him a cup of tea and he joined some of his friends. They greeted him NOISILY.

Exercise 9.6 Practice expressions of Manner.

Examples: Teacher	Student
What did Mr. Tower say on the phone?	He said, "Thank you very much."
Was he on time?	No, he was late.
How did his eyes close?	They closed slowly.

---

*"Répondez s'il vous plaît," "Please respond."

1. How did he dress?
2. How was Mrs. Price waiting?
3. How did Mr. Tower speak to the hostess?

4. Didn't he speak rudely?
5. How did she answer him?
6. Did his friends greet him quietly?

≡ E.   Observe -ER and -OR.

Robert: What do "WORKER" and "ACTOR" mean?

Edward: "Worker" means a person who works and "actor" means a man who acts.

Exercise 9.7   Practice -ER and -OR.

Examples: Teacher   Student

What is a person who teaches?   He's a teacher.
What is a person who teaches   He's a history teacher.
    history?

1. What is a person who plays tennis?
2. What is a person who plays chess?
3. What is a person who drives a taxi?
4. What is a person who drives a bus?
5. What is a person who writes stories?
6. What is a person who reports news?
7. What is a person who sings opera?

8   What is a person who dances ballet?
9. What is a thing that plays records?
10. What is a thing that sharpens pencils?

Summary Dialogue.

I met an old friend in town yesterday. He was with his mother-in-law. After introductions we went to a restaurant for a cup of coffee.

His mother-in-law asked me, "When did you meet my son-in-law?"

I said, "I met him seven years ago. We knew each other during our high school days. After high school I joined the army."

"When did you get back?"

"I arrived at the airport last Saturday evening and got to my brother's house the next morning."

Homework.

Write about one of your experiences. Use: GET, KNOW, Directions and some words with -LY and -ER endings.

Lesson X

A. Review questions.
B. General review.
C. AT, ON, IN, INTO, etc.

☰ A.1[1]   1. Good morning. How are you?
2. Where are you from?
3. What's your name?
4. What is your phone number?
5. What are you?
6. What is she?
7. Are you a lawyer?
8. Are you hungry?
9. Is he sleepy?
10. What time is it?
11. What day is it?
12. When is your birthday?
13. Where's your book?
14. Where are we?

☰ A.2   1. Where do you live?
2. What do you do during the day?
3. When do you study?
4. Don't you ever study at night?
5. When do you eat?
6. How do you eat dinner?
7. What kind of pie do you like?
8. What kind of pie would you like?
9. What do you want?
10. How much is a piece of pie and a glass of milk?
11. Do you have change for a ten?
12. What kind of change do you have?
13. Don't you like cold weather?
14. Do you study every night?

☰ A.3   1. How much money did you have last week?
2. What did you do yesterday?
3. When did you study?
4. What did you do today?
5. What did you eat yesterday?
6. When was the weather warm?
7. When did you arrive?
8. What did you do last year?
9. Did you speak English every day last week?
10. Did you study all day yesterday?
11. What did you do before lunch? (Use: Time expressions.)
12. What did you do after lunch?
13. Were you late to class this morning?
14. Which city were you near last Sunday?

☰ A.4   1. Where do you live now?
2. What were you doing this noon?
3. Where were you sleeping last night?
4. What are you doing now?
5. Where were you going this morning?
6. Where were you going last Saturday?
7. Which lesson are we studying?
8. Which book were you reading?
9. Were you going to the laundry last Saturday morning?
10. What are you studying now?

NOTE TO TEACHER: [1]Each section corresponds to a lesson; A.1 reviews Lesson 1, etc.

71

≡ A.5   1. What are you going to do   6. What are you going to buy at
           tomorrow?   the drugstore?
        2. What are you going to do   7. Where are you going to live
           next week?   next semester?
        3. Where are you going   8. Aren't you going to be here
           Saturday?   three months?
        4. When does your bus leave?   9. What are you going to do
        5. When are you coming back?   during the weekend?

≡ A.6   1. (Touching hand) Is this my   8. How much money are you going
           arm?   to spend?
        2. (Showing finger) What is   9. What do you sometimes miss?
           this?   10. What do you often lose?
        3. What am I wearing?   11. What do you always waste?
        4. What are you wearing?   12. How far did you drive last
        5. What did you wear to the   weekend?
           program last Friday night? 13. How long did you drive last
        6. What did your girl friend   weekend?
           wear?   14. Are you going shopping
        7. What are you going to buy   tomorrow?
           at the store? (Use: 15. How long did this exercise
           A FEW, etc.)   take?

≡ A.7   1. Who are you taking to the   7. What do you comb your hair
           party tomorrow night?   with?
        2. What is her name?   8. Who is your father's son?
        3. What did you make yesterday? 9. Who is your mother-in-law's
        4. What did you do yesterday?   daughter?
           (Use: DO.)   10. What is usually around a
        5. When are you free?   house?
        6. What do you do before a   11. What kind of furniture is in
           date?   a living room?
                                        12. What kind of furniture is in
                                            your room?

≡ A.8   1. What did you borrow from   5. What did the boy and his sister
           your roommate last week?   enter at the park?
        2. What did your classmate   6. What did they watch?
           lend you last week?   7. What did they attend?
        3. What happened to Jack at the 8. What did they enjoy?
           movies last Saturday?   9. Did Professor Reed sleep on the
        4. What did Betty write to her   ice?
           brother about?

≡ A.9   1. When did you get here?   6. Where is the dormitory?
        2. What did you get yesterday?   7. How do I get there?
        3. Why did Pete come home?   8. Where is the United States?
           (Use: GET.)   9. Where are its large cities?
        4. Are you acquainted with him? 10. How do you usually talk?
        5. When did you meet him?   (Use: -LY.)

≡ B.[1]　　General Review.

1. What do people say during an introduction?

2. Describe your activities today. Use: THIS MORNING, THIS
   NOON, AT EIGHT O'CLOCK, etc.

3. Describe your activities yesterday.

4. Describe a friend. Use: TALL, SHORT, OLD, YOUNG, etc.

5. Describe your room. Use: DESK, CHAIR, TABLE LAMP, etc.;
   IN, ON, NEAR, etc.

6. a. Describe your friend's clothes. Use: WEAR, BLUE, BROWN,
      SLACKS, SUIT, etc.
   b. Describe the human body and its functions.

7. a. Describe your home.
   b. Describe your family. Use: MOTHER, FATHER, COUSIN,
      etc.

8. Describe one of your past experiences. For example: A Date,
   A Letter, A Trip to the Zoo, etc.

9. a. Describe a walk downtown. Use: OUT OF, ACROSS,
      THROUGH, ALONG, etc.
   b. Direct one of your classmates around the room. Use:
      RIGHT, LEFT, STRAIGHT AHEAD, etc.; TURN, CROSS, etc.

≡ C.1　AT, ON, and IN sometimes indicate *time* and *address*.

John came here	AT	six o'clock,
	ON	Tuesday, May first,
	IN	1964.
He is living	AT	106 (Hill Street),
	ON	Hill Street,
	IN	New York.

NOTE: AT indicates a "point."

NOTE TO TEACHER: [1]Question 1 reviews Lesson 1, etc.

Exercise 10.1 Practice AT, ON, and IN: *time.*

Examples:	Teacher	Student
	January	He left in January.
	5:15	He left at 5:15.
	March 3	He left on March third.

1.	1950	5.	the afternoon	9.	Sunday morning
2.	Monday	6.	night	10.	the day before yesterday
3.	June	7.	April 15	11.	last Friday
4.	June 8	8.	10 o'clock	12.	a week ago

Exercise 10.2 Practice AT, ON, IN: *addresses.*

Examples:	Teacher	Student
	home	She lives at home now.
	Chicago	She lives in Chicago now.

1.	Main Street	6.	the Friends Co-op
2.	the hotel	7.	home
3.	downtown	8.	here
4.	Florida	9.	Mexico City
5.	426 Park Street	10.	the dormitory

≡ C.2 AT, ON, IN, INTO, etc. sometimes indicate *location* and *direction.*

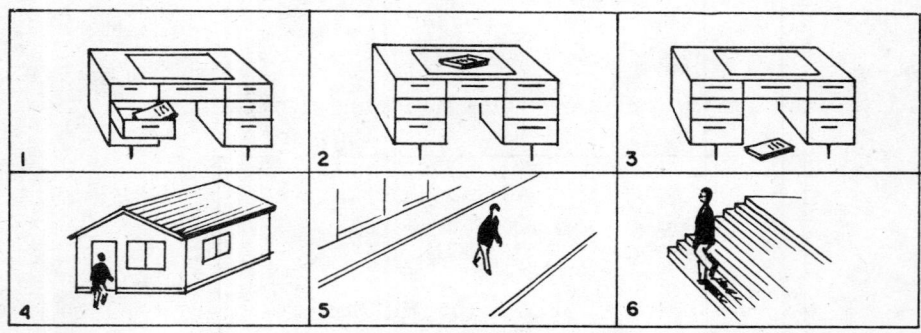

1. Where's the book?	1. It's . . . (in the drawer)
2. Where's the book now?	2. It's . . . (on the desk)
3. Where's the book now?	3. It's . . . (under the desk)
4. Where's he going?	4. He's going . . . (into the house)
5. Where's he going now?	5. He's going . . . (across the street)
6. Where's he going now?	6. He's going . . . (down the stairs)

Exercise 10.3   Practice AT, ON, IN, etc.: *location.*

Examples: <u>Teacher</u>   <u>Student</u>

    Where's your money? (wallet)   My money's in my wallet.
    Where're the lights? (ceiling)   The lights're on the ceiling.
    Where's the table? (light)   The table's under the light.

1. Where's your pen? (pocket)
2. Where're you sitting? (desk)
3. Where am I sitting? (table)
4. Where're your feet? (floor)
5. Where's the window? (wall)

6. Where's Mr. A? (Mr. B)
7. Where's Mr. B? (Mr. A and Mr. C)
8. Where do you do your homework? (the library)
9. Where does Miss Green teach? (the university)

Exercise 10.4   Practice INTO, etc: *direction.*

Examples: <u>Teacher</u>   <u>Student</u>

    What did you come out of this   I came out of my house.
      morning?
    What did you go down?   I went down the steps.

1. What did you go through?
2. What did you go across?
3. What did you go into?
4. What did you go through?
5. What did you come out of?

6. What did you go past?
7. What did you walk along?
8. What did you go up?
9. What did you go into?
10. What did you do then?

≡ C.3   AT, TO, etc. sometimes follow certain verbs.

The children	LISTENED	TO	the birds.
	LOOKED	AT	the flowers.
	LAUGHED	AT	the monkeys.
	TALKED	ABOUT	the animals.
	THOUGHT	ABOUT	their parents.
	WROTE	ABOUT	their experiences.

Exercise 10.5   Practice AT, TO, etc. with LOOK, LISTEN, etc.

Example: <u>Teacher</u>   <u>Student</u>

    think . . . our cousins   We thought about our cousins.

1. look . . . the map of the city
2. listen . . . the music
3. talk . . . the animals at the Zoo
4. laugh . . . the joke

5. think . . . our grandmother
6. write . . . our little brother
7. listen . . . the radio

☰ C.4 Verbs with ON, INTO, etc. sometimes form *a single unit*. We call
these "two-word" verbs.

(Please look at the pictures on page 77.)

Picture 1. What's he doing?   1. He's...(PUTTING ON his tie)
Picture 2. What's he doing?   2. He's...(TAKING OFF his overcoat)
Picture 3. What're his friends   3. They're...(CALLING ON them)
                doing?
Picture 4. What's he doing?   4. He's...(LOOKING UP a word)
Picture 5. What's she doing?   5. She's (LOOKING FOR something)
Picture 6. What's she doing?   6. She's...(PICKING UP her groceries)
Picture 7. What's he doing?   7. He's...(CALLING UP his girl friend)
Picture 8. What did he do?   8. He...(RAN INTO some friends)
Picture 9. What did she do?   9. She...(RAN OUT OF money)

Exercise 10.6 Practice Two-word Verbs.

Example: Teacher   Student

        Is the man in Picture 1 taking   No, he's putting it on.
          off his tie?

1. Is the man in Picture 2 putting on his overcoat?
2. Are the people in Picture 3 calling up their friends?
3. Picture 4. Is he picking up a word?
4. Picture 5. Is she looking up something in her purse?
5. Picture 6. Is she looking up her groceries?
6. Picture 7. Is he calling on his girl friend?
7. Picture 8. Did he run out of friends in town today?
8. Picture 9. Did she run into money at the grocery store?

TWO-WORD VERBS

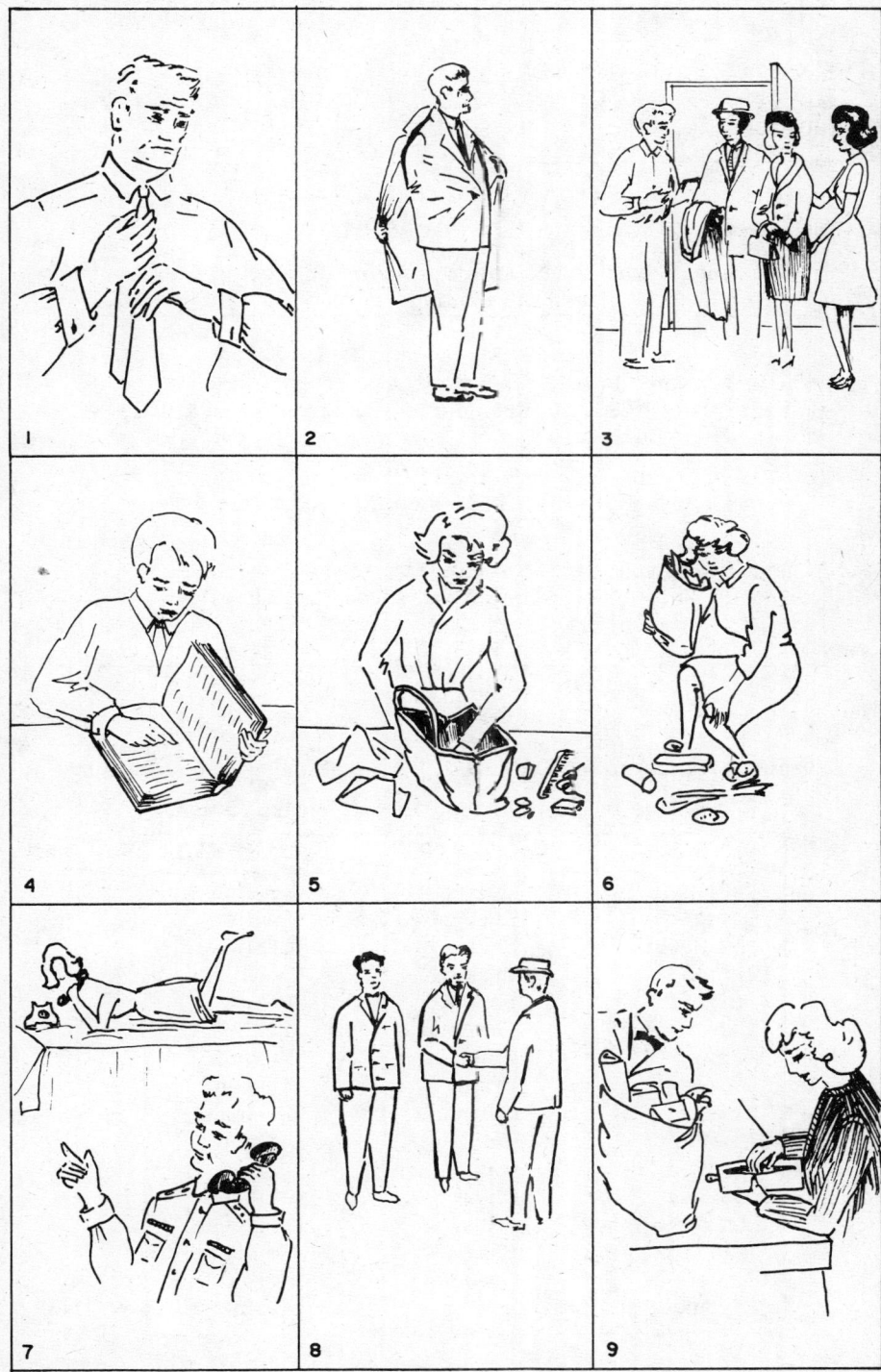

Lesson XI

A. CAN.
B. MAY.
C. MIGHT.
D. SHOULD.

E. MUST.
F. WILL.
G. WOULD RATHER.
H. SHALL.

≡ A. Observe CAN, CAN'T, COULD, COULDN'T.

Situation: Pedro meets an Iraqi student in front of the classroom building.

> Pedro: How do you do? My name is Pedro Saso.
> Ali: My name is Ali. CAN you speak Arabic?
> Pedro: No, I CAN'T. I can only speak Spanish and a little English.
>
> Ali: Where did you study English?
> Pedro: At a high school in Mexico City about four years ago.
>
> Ali: Didn't you learn to speak it well?
> Pedro: Yes. I COULD read and speak English fairly well then, but I can't now.

NOTE: CAN indicates *ability*.

Exercise 11.1 Practice CAN, CAN'T. First observe the following:

Pedro Saso is from Mexico. He can speak Spanish.

PERSON	COUNTRY	LANGUAGE
Pedro	Mexico	Spanish
Dave	The United States	English
Mr. Harris	England	English
Ahmet	Turkey	Turkish
Jan	Poland	Polish
Manat	Thailand	Thai
Karri	Finland	Finnish
Pierre	France	French
Ernst	Germany	German
Antonio	Italy	Italian
Mr. Zivari	Iran	Persian
Mr. Lee	China	Chinese
Mr. Saito	Japan	Japanese
Joao	Brazil	Portuguese
Demetrius	Greece	Greek
Farouk	Iraq	Arabic

Examples: Teacher   Student

       Bob is from Detroit   A. Can he speak Greek?
                                     B. No, he can't. He can only
                                              speak English.

       José is from Venezuela.   C. Can he speak Polish?
                                     D. No, he can't. He can only
                                              speak Spanish.

       Karl is from Germany.   E. Can he speak Chinese?
                                     F. No, he can't. He can only
                                              speak German.

1. Pierre is from France.   6. Ahmet is from Turkey.
2. Jack is from Miami.   7. Antonio is from Italy.
3. Alfredo is from Brazil.   8. Mr. Ogawa is from Japan.
4. Mr. Lee is from China.   9. Rosa is from Peru.
5. Mr. Amin is from Iran.   10. Manat is from Thailand.

≡ B. Observe MAY.

    Situation: Pedro enters the English Office.

Secretary: MAY I help you?
Pedro: Yes, please. May I speak with Mr. Norris?
Secretary: I'm sorry, he's busy right now. He will be free
              in a few minutes.

Pedro: I'll wait. May I smoke?
Secretary: Yes, and you may also look at those maga-
              zines.

NOTE: MAY indicates *permission*.[1]

Exercise 11.2   Practice MAY in questions of permission.

Examples: Teacher   Student

   speak Spanish in class   A. May I speak Spanish in class?
                                    B. No, you may not.

   have your phone number   A. May I have your phone number?
                                     B. Yes, you may.

   smoke in class   A. May I smoke in class?
                                     B. No, you may not.

1. open the window   5. have a piece of lemon pie
2. ask a question   6. have another cup of coffee
3. speak French in class   7. look at your pictures
4. speak with the director   8. close the door

NOTE TO TEACHER: [1]CAN is often used to express permission in
informal situations; e.g., "Can I help you?" "Can I smoke?"

☰ C. Observe MIGHT.

Situation: Pedro sits down beside a Japanese student.

Pedro: Which university are you going to?
Koichi: I'm not sure. I MIGHT go to the University of California or
      I might stay here.

Pedro: How many courses will you take the first term?
Koichi: I'm not certain. I might take four.

Secretary: Mr. Norris can see you now.
Pedro: Excuse me. I might see you at the dorm for dinner.
Koichi: So long.

NOTE: MIGHT indicates *possibility*.

Exercise 11.3   Practice MIGHT

Examples: <u>Teacher</u>   <u>Student</u>

What are you going to do tonight?
    go to the movies

                                      I don't know. I might go to the
                                           movies.

    study in the lab   I don't know. I might study in
                                         the lab.

1. go skating	6. play chess
2. go on a date	7. go bowling
3. read some magazines	8. attend a lecture
4. make a cake	9. visit my friends
5. call up my girl friend	10. study my lessons

☰ D. Observe SHOULD.

Situation: Pedro is speaking to Mr. Norris.

Pedro: SHOULD I bring my passport to registration tomorrow?
Mr. Norris: Yes, you should.

Pedro: I have a little problem. I lost the key to my locker and my
    passport is inside.
Mr. Norris: You should try to find the key.

Pedro: Yes, sir. One more thing. Where can I get a list of the books
    for my English course?
Mr. Norris: You should go to the office on the second floor.

NOTE: SHOULD indicates *propriety, duty, obligation*.

Exercise 11.4 Practice SHOULD.

Examples: <u>Teacher</u>   <u>Student</u>

    the dentist   A. What did the dentist tell you?
                   B. He told me I should brush my teeth
                      every day.

    the doctor   C. What did the doctor tell you?
                   D. He told me I should drink more milk.

    the grammar   E. What did the grammar teacher tell you?
      teacher   F. He told me I should study every day.

    1. your sister   6. the librarian
    2. your mother   7. your aunt
    3. your father   8. your mother-in-law
    4. your roommate   9. your brother
    5. your girl friend   10. your cousin

≡ E. Observe MUST.

    Situation: Pedro is talking to the secretary in the office.

> Pedro: Hello. May I have a list of the English books?
> Secretary: Surely. You're from Mexico, aren't you?
> Pedro: Yes, that's right.
> Secretary: Then you MUST speak Spanish.

NOTE: MUST indicates a *logical inference*.

Exercise 11.5   Practice MUST.

Examples: <u>Teacher</u>   <u>Student</u>

The doctor worked hard today.   He must be tired.
The students study every day.   They must know a lot of English.

    1. Marie always gets good grades.
    2. Henry is smiling.
    3. The teacher is yawning.
    4. Pierre is from France.
    5. Chuck goes to the library every night.
    6. Nancy is going to the bank this noon.
    7. Mr. Sato is from Japan.
    8. Manat is from Thailand.
    9. Demetrius is from Greece.

☰ F.   Observe WILL (I'LL).

Situation: Pedro is walking back to the dorm with a Venezuelan student.

Alfonso: Did you find the key to your locker?
Pedro: No, I didn't.

Alfonso: What WILL you do?
Pedro: I'll speak to my adviser.

Alfonso: Can you go to the movies tonight?
Pedro: I WON'T know until later. I'll call you up at five o'clock.

NOTE: WILL indicates future time. The negative is WON'T.

Exercise 11.6   Practice WILL.

Examples: Teacher   Student

I didn't see my adviser yesterday.
          today   A. Will you see him today?
                                    B. No, I won't.
                                    A. When will you see him?
          next week   B. I'll see him next week.

I didn't do my homework
   last night
          tonight   C. Will you do it tonight?
                                    D. No, I won't.
                                    C. When will you do it?
       during the weekend   D. I'll do it during the
                                             weekend.

       1. I didn't see the doctor yesterday afternoon.
             this afternoon
             tomorrow afternoon
       2. I didn't buy my books today.
             tomorrow
             on Thursday
       3. I didn't go to the barbershop last Saturday.
             this Saturday
             a week from this Saturday
       4. I didn't write to my parents yesterday.
             tonight
             the day after tomorrow
       5. I didn't wash my clothes yesterday morning.
             this afternoon
             Saturday morning

≡ G. Observe WOULD RATHER (I'D RATHER).

Situation: Pedro discusses his problem with his adviser.

Pedro: May I speak to you a minute?
Mr. Kelly: Yes, certainly.

Pedro: I can't find the key to my locker.
Mr. Kelly: Then you must break your lock. WOULD you
RATHER borrow some tools or call the janitor?

Pedro: I'd rather borrow some tools.
Mr. Kelly: All right. Let's get a hammer and a screw driver
for you.

NOTE: WOULD RATHER indicates a *preference*.

Exercise 11.7   Practice WOULD RATHER.

Examples:	Teacher	Student

What would you rather have?
   hot chocolate or tea   I'd rather have tea.
   apple pie or banana cake   I'd rather have apple pie.

1. steak or chicken
2. an apple or an orange
3. meat and potatoes or meat
and rice
4. a cup of coffee or a cup of
tea
5. a piece of cake or a piece of
pie

6. a glass of milk or a glass of
beer
7. a slice of bread or a loaf of
bread
8. a dish of ice cream or a quart of
ice cream
9. a bowl of soup or a bowl of soap
10. a date with Joan or a date with
John

≡ H.   Observe SHALL.

Situation: Pedro and his roommate are in their room.

Pedro: What SHALL I do first?
Guy: Why don't you look for your key again?

Pedro: It's very warm in here. Shall I open the window?
Guy: Yes, please do.

Pedro: Where should I look? In my coin purse?

Guy: Why not?
Pedro: Well, what do you know. Here it is.

Exercise 11.8   Practice questions with SHALL.

Examples: <u>Teacher</u>   <u>Student</u>

      go to the movies   A. Shall we go to the movies?

                        B. Yes, let's. (or) No, let's not.

1. put on our new suits   6. wear our new ties
2. go to a movie   7. sing some songs
3. shave   8. play cards
4. have dinner downtown   9. go bowling
5. study together   10. go swimming

Exercise 11.9   Summary exercise.

Examples: Teacher   Student

Indicate ability . . . speak English   He can speak English.
Indicate possibility . . . call on Mary   He might call on Mary.
Indicate obligation . . . study tonight   He should study tonight.

1. possibility. . . . . visit Chicago
2. ability . . . . not go last night
3. logical inference . . . be tired
4. obligation. . . . . practice a lot
5. permission. . . . . . . smoke here
6. ability . . . . not skate very well
7. obligation. . . . . pick up the papers
8. possibility . . . . run out of money
9. preference . . . . call up Sally
10. logical inference . . . swim well
11. future . . . . put on my new shirt
12. possibility . . . . run into Bill
13. obligation. . . . . take off his hat

Review questions.

1. How many languages can you speak?   6. What language must
2. How many languages could you   Pierre speak?
    speak five years ago?   7. When will you see your
3. May we speak Spanish in class?   girl friend?
4. What might you do this evening?   8. Would you rather drink
5. What should a student always do?   coffee, or tea?
                                 9. Shall we have an examina-
                                   tion tomorrow?

Lesson XII

A. LOOK UP, PUT ON, TAKE OFF, etc.
B. Men's Clothing Sizes; COUPLE, PAIR.
C. INTEND, TRY.
D. PASS, SPEND.

☰ A. Observe LOOK UP, PICK UP, etc.

Situation: Ken and Jim are in their room after dinner.

Ken: What's our homework assignment for chemistry?
Jim: Just a minute. I'll LOOK it UP in my notebook.

Ken: I think I'll TAKE OFF this heavy shirt. Did you CALL
      UP your girl friend this afternoon?
Jim: Yes, I called her up, but I wasn't able to talk to her.
      She HUNG UP.

Ken: She must still be angry with you.
Jim: Here's the assignment. We have to read Chapter
      Nine.

Ken: Good! I read that chapter this morning. I think I'll
      PUT ON a clean shirt, PICK UP my suit at the
      cleaners, and PICK UP Ann. She wants to TRY
      ON some new hats.

Exercise 12.1 Practice LOOK UP, PICK UP, etc.

Example: Teacher   Student

a. What did Jim look up in his   He looked up the homework
     notebook?   assignment.

   1. What did Ken take off?   5. What did he pick up at the
   2. Who did Jim call up?   cleaners?
   3. Did he hang up?   6. Who did he pick up?
   4. Did Ken put on a dirty shirt? 7. What did Ann want to do?

b. 1. What do you often look up?   6. What do you need to pick
    2. What do you always take off?   up this afternoon?
    3. Who do you like to call up?   7. Will you pick up your girl
    4. Who usually hangs up?   friend tonight?
    5. What do you like to put on?   8. What do women like to try
                                        on?

≡ B.1   Observe Men's Clothing Sizes;   LEATHER, DRESS SHIRT, etc.

Situation: At a department store. Ann is in the Women's Wear
Department, and Jim is in the Men's Wear
Department. A salesman speaks to Jim.

Salesman: Good morning, Sir. May I help you?
Jim: Yes. I'd like to buy a light gray TWEED suit.
Salesman: What SIZE do you wear?
Jim: Size 38 LONG.

Salesman: Here you are. What kind of BELT would you like?
Jim: I'd like a black LEATHER one. My waist is 34 INCHES.

Salesman: Do you like this one?
Jim: Yes, that will be fine. Next, I need a NARROW
BRIMMED hat.

Salesman: Let's see. This one is size $7\frac{1}{8}$. It should fit you.
Jim: It's a perfect fit.

Salesman: Will there be anything else?
Jim: Well, I could use a blue DRESS SHIRT with a BUTTON-
DOWN COLLAR. My neck is size 15 and my arm
length is 34.

Salesman: Are you interested in shoes today?
Jim: Yes, I should get a pair of LOAFERS. Do you carry
Italian shoes? I wear size 10C.

Salesman: Yes, we do.
Jim: I also need some socks—size 12.

NOTES: CLOTHING sizes are usually measured in inches.
SPORT SHIRT sizes are S(small), M(medium), L(large).
SHOE sizes: 10 refers to length, C refers to medium
width.
SOCKS are about two sizes larger than shoes.
SUIT sizes: 38 long is for a tall man, 38 short is
for a short man.

Exercise 12.2   Practice Men's Clothing Sizes.

Examples: Teacher   Student

Why did Jim go to the Men's
Wear Department?
               8B   He went to buy some shoes.
               $7\frac{3}{8}$ He went to buy a hat.

1. 38 short	5. $11\frac{1}{2}$	9. $6\frac{7}{8}$
2. 32	6. $7\frac{1}{2}$B	10. $10\frac{1}{2}$C
3. 10D	7. 33	11. 12E
4. 15-33	8. 42 long	12. medium

≡ B.2   Observe COUPLE, PAIR.

> Situation: Jim and Ann are leaving the department store.

> Jim: What did you buy?
> Ann: I bought a COUPLE of blouses, a couple of skirts,
>   three PAIRS of NYLONS, a pair of high-heel shoes,
>   and a pair of pajamas.
>
> Jim: Did you charge them or pay cash?
> Ann: Neither. I gave the saleslady a check for them.

NOTES: COUPLE usually means *two*.
        PAIR is for things with two similar parts.

Exercise 12.3   Practice COUPLE and PAIR.

Examples: Teacher   Student

> What did Ann buy?
>   shoes   She bought a pair of shoes.
>   dresses   She bought a couple of dresses.

1. slacks   4. sleeveless sweaters   7. earrings
2. handkerchiefs   5. blouses   8. pins
3. sunglasses   6. brown low-heel shoes   9. pajamas
                                                10. nylons

≡ C.   Observe INTEND and TRY.

> Situation: Ann and Jim are in front of a hardware store.

> Jim: What do you plan to do this afternoon?
> Ann: First, I INTEND to take off these high-heel shoes.
>   Then, I intend to clean house and take a short nap.
>   What are you going to do?
>
> Jim: I'm going to TRY to finish my homework assignment.
>   It's very difficult.
> Ann: Good luck!

NOTES: INTEND expresses *plan*.
       TRY expresses *make an effort*.

Exercise 12.4   Practice INTEND and TRY.

Examples:	Teacher	Student
	Jim and Ann were engaged. (get married)	They intended to get married.
	Harry lost a quarter. (find it)	He tried to find it.

1. Carol couldn't cook very well. (make a cake)
2. Mr. Clark needed a new suit. (buy one)
3. Pedro didn't speak English well. (pronounce correctly)
4. Mrs. Clark invited some friends for dinner. (serve chicken)
5. He couldn't pronounce *r*. (imitate the teacher)
6. Mrs. Taylor needed a new dress. (go shopping)
7. He forgot my address. (find it in the phone book)
8. Jim didn't write a check. (pay cash)

☰ D.   Observe PASS and SPEND.

Situation: Ken is in his classmate's room after dinner.

> Ken: Did you PASS your math final yesterday?
> Dave: Yes, I got 85 on it.
>
> Ken: I PASSED the bulletin board near the math department this morning, but I didn't see any grades on it.
> Dave: Our instructor seldom puts them up on the bulletin board.
>
> Ken: Please hand me the phone. I want to call up my girl friend.
> Dave: Here you are.
>
> Ken: Hi, Sue. How are you? How much time did you SPEND on your paper today?
> Sue: I only spent two hours. Marian asked me to go shopping with her.
>
> Ken: You'll never finish your paper that way. Did you SPEND all of your money?
> Sue: No, I have a quarter left.

Exercise 12.5 Practice PASS and SPEND.

Examples:	Teacher	Student
	What did you do?	
	a few days in Chicago	I spent a few days in Chicago.
	$10 last weekend	I spent $10 last weekend.
	the sugar	I passed the sugar.

1. the salt
2. a couple of weeks in New York
3. him a napkin
4. eight hours at the office
5. my vacation in Europe
6. all my money
7. the English examination
8. $1.50 for a pair of socks
9. five hours in class
10. your house yesterday

Summary Dialogue.

Charles: Why did Old Frank go to that country?
Richard: He went for two reasons: for his health and in order to get rich.

Charles: Did he succeed?
Richard: Yes and no. He made a lot of money by working hard, but he lost it all by spending it foolishly.

Charles: Well, that's life.

Review questions.

1. Who did you call up last night?
2. When did you put on your best suit?
3. What did you pick up for your friend?
4. What did you try on last week?
5. What do you usually look up in a dictionary?
6. What size belt did you buy?
7. What size shoes did you get?
8. What did you pass last weekend?
9. What did you spend last weekend?
10. What do you intend to do tomorrow?
11. What did you try to do yesterday?

Lesson XIII

A. TAKE.
B. EXPECT, HOPE, WAIT FOR.
C. HAVE TO, BE ABLE TO, OUGHT TO.
D. HAVE GOT.

≡ A.   Observe TAKE.

Situation: Mr. Black meets his neighbor, Mr. Hunter, near
the bookstore.

Mr. Black: Shall we TAKE A WALK around the block?
Mr. Hunter: Yes, let's. It's a beautiful day.

Mr. Black: Yes, it is. I see you're interested in history.
Mr. Hunter: No, I bought this book for my son. He's
TAKING A COURSE in American history.
He TOOK AN EXAM in it this morning.

Mr. Black: When do you intend to TAKE YOUR VACATION?
Mr. Hunter: In June.

Mr. Black: Didn't you TAKE A TRIP to California last June?
Mr. Hunter: Yes, we did.

Mr. Black: Did you TAKE A PLANE or YOUR CAR?
Mr. Hunter: We took our car. It was a 2000-mile trip
and it TOOK us TWO WEEKS.

Mr. Black: Did you TAKE many PICTURES?
Mr. Hunter: Yes, we did. Why don't you and your wife
come over and see them tonight?[1]
Mr. Black: Thank you. We'll be happy to.

Exercise 13.1   Practice TAKE.

Examples: Teacher	Student
want	A. What did you want to do?
a vacation	B. I wanted to take a vacation.
intend	C. What did you intend to do?
a trip to Japan	D. I intended to take a trip to Japan.

1. plan   4. agree
   a bus to Chicago   a course in English
2. try   5. remember
   a trip in December   a picture of the University
3. need   6. forget
   a walk through the park   an examination

NOTE TO TEACHER: [1]WHY DON'T YOU . . . sometimes expresses
an informal invitation.

Exercise 13.2   Review DO, MAKE, and TAKE.

Examples: Teacher	Student
How did you get to Ann Arbor? (a plane)	I got to Ann Arbor by taking a plane.
How did you succeed? (progress)	I succeeded by making progress.

1. How did you get to Chicago? (a bus)
2. How did you learn English? (a course in English)
3. How did you meet Mary? (a date with her best friend)
4. How did you pass the course? (my homework every night)

5. How did you intend to get rich? (a lot of money)
6. How did you plan to spend your money? (a trip to Europe)
7. How did you forget your dentist appointment? (a walk through the park)
8. How did you meet Barbara? (a favor for her cousin)

≡ B.   Observe EXPECT, HOPE, WAIT FOR.

Situation: Mr. and Mrs. Hunter are in their living room after dinner. Mr. Hunter looks at his watch.

Mrs. H: Are you EXPECTING someone, dear?
Mr. H: Yes, our neighbors. I promised to show them the slides of our trip tonight.

Mrs. H: I HOPE you won't show them all of your slides.
Mr. H: No, I won't. I'll only show them the best ones.

Mrs. H: How long must[1] we WAIT FOR them?
Mr. H: I don't know. They are fifteen minutes late now.

NOTES: EXPECT means *feel sure* or *believe* that an event will occur.
HOPE includes the idea of a wish or a desire.

Exercise 13.3   Practice WAIT FOR and HOPE.

Examples: Teacher	Student
	A. What are we waiting for?
the six o'clock train	B. We're waiting for the six o'clock train.
on time	A. I hope it gets here on time.
	B. I hope so, too.

1. a bus
   soon
2. a streetcar
   in a few minutes
3. the afternoon train
   soon

4. the next bus
   in a few minutes
5. the four o'clock bus
   on time

NOTE TO TEACHER: [1]MUST here means *necessity.*

Exercise 13.4   Practice EXPECT.

Examples: Teacher   Student

I am studying hard. (learn English)   I expect to learn English.
I'm going to work 8 hours today.   I expect to be tired tonight.
  (be tired tonight)

1. I am 10,000 miles from my home. (get homesick)
2. I see my friend after class every day. (see him today)
3. My friend said, "I'll be back very soon." (see him in a few minutes)
4. I will finish my studies in May. (get a degree)
5. I get a letter every week. (get one next Tuesday)

≡ C.1   Observe HAVE TO.

Situation: Everyone is looking at Mr. Hunter's color slides.

> Mr. Black: Where did you take this picture?
> Mr. Hunter: At the hotel in Yosemite National Park.
>
> Mr. Black: Was it necessary to reserve your hotel room?
> Mr. Hunter: Yes, we HAD TO make our reservations two
>   months in advance.

NOTE: HAVE TO indicates *necessity*.

Exercise 13.5   Practice HAVE TO in past time expressions.

Examples: Teacher   Student

Couldn't Dave go to the movies   No, he had to study.
  last night? (study)
Couldn't he come to the picnic   No, he had to go to Detroit.
  today? (go to Detroit)

1. Couldn't he say yes? (nod his head)
2. Couldn't he say no? (shake his head)
3. Couldn't he wait for his friend? (see his teacher)
4. Couldn't he take some pictures? (buy a roll of film)
5. Couldn't he take a trip? (work)
6. Couldn't he sit down? (stand up)
7. Couldn't he go to the concert? (study for an examination)

≡ C.2   Observe BE ABLE TO.

> Mr. Hunter: Here are some pictures of San Francisco.
> Mr. Black: Where's the Golden Gate Bridge?
>
> Mr. Hunter: We should BE ABLE TO see it in this picture,
>   but we can't. It's behind those buildings.

NOTE: BE ABLE TO expresses *ability*.

Exercise 13.6   Practice BE ABLE TO.[1]

Examples: Teacher	Student

I was busy all day.
    call up Mary
    pick up my laundry
	I wasn't able to call up Mary.
	I wasn't able to pick up my
	    laundry.

1. I worked hard last night.
    look up the new words
    pick up my girl friend

2. I spent five hours at the
    dentist's yesterday.
    do my homework
    visit my friend

3. June had to study yesterday.
    play tennis
    watch television

4. Marge had to work last
    night.
      come to the party
      go to the play

≡ C.3   Observe OUGHT TO.

> Mr. Black: Thank you for the show. Your slides are excellent.
> Mr. Hunter: You're quite welcome. You really OUGHT TO visit
>   California.
>
> Mr. Black: Yes, I know we ought to. In fact, we should take our
>   children to many parts of the United States.

NOTE: OUGHT TO indicates *duty, obligation, propriety.*

Exercise 13.7   Practice OUGHT TO.

Examples: Teacher	Student
I didn't write to my parents last week.	You ought to write to them this week.
I didn't do my homework last night.	You ought to do it tonight.

1. I didn't attend class yesterday.
2. I didn't study last night.
3. I didn't wash my clothes last
    Saturday.
4. I didn't review the first ten
    lessons last night.

5. I didn't take a vacation
    last year.
6. I didn't go to bed early
    last night.
7. I didn't shave yesterday.
8. I didn't put on my new
    sweater this morning.

NOTE TO TEACHER: [1]BE ABLE TO may be used after <u>will</u>, <u>should</u>, etc. and in sentences like "I would like to BE ABLE TO sing," "You're going to BE ABLE TO speak English." (CAN is not used after auxiliaries or after <u>to</u>.)

☰ D.   Observe HAVE GOT.

Situation: Mr. and Mrs. Black are talking together.

Mrs. Black: I enjoyed the slides very much.
Mr. Black: So did I. He'S certainly GOT some beautiful
            pictures.

Mrs. Black: Yes, he has. Incidentally, when do we have to
            visit your family?
Mr. Black: We'VE GOT to visit them next Sunday.

Mrs. Black: It seems late. HAVE you GOT the correct
            time?
Mr. Black: Yes, it's 11:15.

NOTE: HAVE GOT indicates *possession* and *necessity*.

Exercise 13.8   Practice HAVE GOT.

Examples: Teacher   Student

What have you got in your pocket?   I've got a pen in my pocket.
What have I got in my hand?   You've got a book in your hand.

1. Have you got a pen in your shirt pocket?
2. Have you got some money in your wallet?
3. What have you got in your pockets?
4. How many pencils have you got?
5. Who's got a dictionary?
6. Have you got the correct time?
7. Have you got a match?
8. Have you got a minute?
9. Have you got any questions?

Review questions.

1. What are some things that you plan to take this year?
2. Are you going to make a date with Susan, or with the doctor?
3. Who are you waiting for?
4. What do you expect to get on the final examination?
5. What are you hoping for?
6. When do you hope to get married?
7. How do you have to study in order to get good grades?
8. What were you able to do this month?
9. Who ought to be able to speak English?

Lesson XIV

A. Seasons, Thermometers.
B. WINDY, FOGGY, DIRTY, etc.
C. REMEMBER, FORGET, REMIND.

≡ A.1 Observe the Seasons.

Situation: Ken and Pablo are having a cup of coffee. They
are talking about the weather.

Pablo: Are there two SEASONS or four seasons in this part of the
United States?
Ken: There are four: SPRING, SUMMER, AUTUMN, and WINTER.

Pablo: We only have two seasons in my country: a rainy one and a
dry one.
Ken: Do you prefer that kind of climate?

Pablo: I don't know. Tell me about the climate here.
Ken: Spring and autumn are the best seasons. In the springtime,
there is a little rain, the grass turns green, and the flowers
begin to bloom. In the fall the leaves turn yellow, orange,
and red and fall from the trees.

Pablo: I suppose winter and summer must be very unpleasant seasons.
Ken: In some ways they are, but in other ways they aren't. It gets
very cold in the wintertime and there's lots of snow, but
many people like winter sports. In the summertime, it's
very hot and often very humid, but many people like to go on
picnics, to have beach parties, and to go swimming.

Pablo: I think I'm going to like this climate.

≡ A.2 The Fahrenheit Thermometer.

Many countries use the Centigrade thermometer. The United States
uses the Fahrenheit thermometer (except in laboratories).

Fahrenheit				Centigrade
	... 212°	WATER BOILS	...	100°
Hot	... 95°		...	35°
Warm	... 65°		...	21°
Cool	... 45°		...	7.3°
Cold	... 32°	WATER FREEZES	...	0°
	... 0°		...	-17.8°

95

Exercise 14.1   Practice the temperature scales.

Example: Teacher   Student

What's thirty-two degrees   It's the same as zero degrees
(32°) Fahrenheit?   (0°) Centigrade.

1. What's 212° Fahrenheit?   1. It's the same as . . . (100° Centigrade)
2. What's   0° F?   2. It's the same as . . . (-17.8° C)
3. What's   45° F?   3. It's the same as . . . (7.3° C)
4. What's   65° F?   4. It's the same as . . . (21° C)
5. What's   95° F?   5. It's the same as . . . (35° C)

Exercise 14.2   Practice SPRING, SUMMER, AUTUMN, WINTER.

Examples: Teacher   Student

What season is July in?   It's in the summer.
When is the temperature 25°?   It's 25° during the winter.

1. What season is January in?   6. When is the temperature about
2. What season is April in?   60°?
3. What season is October in?   7. What happens in the spring?
4. When is the temperature 95°?   8. What happens in the winter?
5. When is the temperature -5°?   9. What happens in the summer?
   (Five degrees below zero.)   10. What happens in the fall?

≡ B.   Observe WINDY, DIRTY, etc.

Pablo: Is it true that there's a lot of wind in Chicago?
Ken: Yes, that's why it's called "the WINDY city."

Pablo: Is it true that there is a lot of dirt in big cities?
Ken: Yes, the streets get very DIRTY and have to be cleaned
        every night.

Pablo: Is it true that San Francisco has a lot of fog?
Ken: Yes, it's true. San Francisco is very FOGGY.

Pablo: Is it true that there is a lot of dust here?
Ken: Yes, it's very DUSTY when the weather is dry.

Exercise 14.3   Practice WINDY, FOGGY, DUSTY, etc.

Examples: Teacher   Student

Is there a lot of ice on the streets?   Yes, it's very icy.
Is the wind strong today?   Yes, it's very windy.
Was there much rain last month?   Yes, it was very rainy.

1. Are there many clouds in the sky?
2. Is there much dirt on your car?
3. Is there much rain during the spring?
4. Is there a lot of dust in the summer?
5. Is the sun shining?
6. Is there much fog in San Francisco?
7. Are there many storms during the winter?
8. Is there a lot of sand in a desert?
9. Is there much wind in Chicago?
10. Is the breeze strong outside?

≡ C.1　　Observe REMEMBER and FORGET.

Ken:	Did you REMEMBER to buy an umbrella?
Pablo:	No, I FORGOT to; but I remembered to buy a pair of rubbers.
Ken:	Can you remember the store I recommended?
Pablo:	No, I can't. Which one was it?
Ken:	Peterson's. It's on Main Street between Fourth and Fifth.

NOTE: REMEMBER means *hold in memory, think of again.*

Exercise 14.4　　Practice REMEMBER and FORGET.

Examples:　　Teacher　　　　　　　　　Student

your doctor appointment　　A. Did you remember your doctor appointment?

date with Joan　　　　　　B. No, I forgot it; but I remembered my date with Joan.

1. to comb your hair
   to brush your teeth
2. the day of the exam
   the time and the place
3. to buy a pen
   to buy some paper

4. the difference between "slipped" and "slept"
   the difference between "make" and "do"
5. to do your homework
   to watch television

≡ C.2　　Observe REMIND . . . TO.

Pablo:	Please REMIND me TO get an umbrella tomorrow. I'm very forgetful.
Ken:	All right. I'll remind you to do that. I'll also remind you to study for your examination. You almost failed last time by forgetting to study.

NOTE: REMIND means *cause another person to remember.*

Exercise 14.5   Practice REMIND . . . TO.

Examples: <u>Teacher</u>   <u>Student</u>

What did your friend remind you to do?
  wear a hat   He reminded me to wear a hat.
  make an appointment with my ad-   He reminded me to make an
    viser   appointment with my adviser.

1. call up my uncle   6. close the window
2. make my bed   7. ask Mary to sing
3. do my homework   8. tell Paul about our experience
4. go to the barbershop for a   9. go to the department store for
   haircut   a new hat
5. take some pictures of my 10. go to the post office for some
   classmates   stamps

≡ C.3   Observe REMIND . . . OF.

Pablo: Ken, you REMIND me OF my oldest brother. He always
        helped me to remember things. He sometimes got mad,
        too.

Ken: (Smiling.) You remind me of my youngest brother, Pedro.
        He's exactly like you. He could never remember anything
        either.

Pablo: You know, sometimes even the weather reminds me of home.

Exercise 14.6   Practice REMIND . . . OF.

Examples: <u>Teacher</u>   <u>Student</u>

the summer here   A. What does the summer here
                                remind you of?
the weather in my country   B. It reminds me of the weather
                                in my country.

my friend   C. Who does my friend remind
                                you of?
his brother   D. He reminds me of his brother.

1. my sister   4. the nurse
     your cousin   my mother
2. the spring rain   5. the architect
     the rainy season in my country   my grandfather
3. the doctor   6. that little girl
     my uncle   my daughter

Review questions.

1. What season is July in?
2. When does it rain a lot?
3. What happens during the winter?
4. What happens in the spring?
5. What are some things that you remember?
6. What did you remind your roommate to do last night?
7. Who does your classmate remind you of?
8. What does the weather here remind you of?

Lesson XV

A. LIKE, LOOK LIKE, LOOK.
B. WHO . . . LOOK LIKE, WHAT . . . LIKE, HOW.
C. Measurements, Dimensions, Weights, Liquid Measures.

☰ A.1   Observe LIKE.

Situation: Bob and Bill are having a snack between classes.

> Bob: Do you want to see a picture of my girl friend?
> Bill: Yes, I'd like to very much. Is she LIKE her mother or like her father?
> Bob: Well, her eyes are blue LIKE her mother's, but her hair is blond LIKE her father's.
> Bill: She's very attractive.

NOTE: LIKE means *similar to* or *in a similar manner*.

Exercise 15.1   Practice LIKE.

Example: Teacher   Student

Joe speaks fast. His father   Joe speaks like his father.
speaks the same way.

1. Jean's eyes are dark brown.   3. Mary's hair is brown.
   Her father's eyes are the same.   Her mother's hair is the same.

2. June dresses expensively.   4. Tom sings very poorly.
   Her sister dresses the same way.   His friend sings the same way.

☰ A.2   Observe LOOK LIKE and LOOK.

Situation: John joins Bob and Bill. Bob asks John a question.

> Bob: Does it LOOK LIKE rain outside?[1]
>
> John: Yes, the sky LOOKS very dark. It'll probably rain in a few minutes.

NOTE TO TEACHER: [1]You will also hear: "Does it look like it's going to rain?"

Exercise 15.2   Practice LOOK LIKE and LOOK.

Examples: Teacher   Student

Does Mr. A look like a busy person?   Yes, he looks busy.
Does Mr. B look sleepy?   Yes, he looks like a
                                           sleepy person.

1. Does Mr. P look like a tired person?
2. Does Mr. F's suit look like an expensive one?
3. Does Miss B look like an intelligent person?
4. Do the students look like busy people?
5. Does it look like a windy day?
6. Does Mr. K's watch look expensive?
7. Does Mr. J's car look new?
8. Does Mrs. R look happy?
9. Does Mr. T look successful?
10. Does it look cloudy?

≡ B. Observe WHO . . . LOOK LIKE, WHAT . . . LIKE, and HOW.

Situation: John looks at the picture of Bob's girl friend.

John: WHO does your girl friend LOOK LIKE, Bob?
Bob: I think she resembles both her mother and her
       father. She has her mother's eyes and com-
       plexion, but she has her father's nose and hair.

John: WHAT is she LIKE?
Bob: She's serious and intelligent, but she has her
       father's sense of humor.

John: Didn't she have a cold last week? HOW is she now?
Bob: She's much better, thanks.

NOTES: LOOK LIKE refers to physical appearance. LIKE
refers to general description. HOW with BE refers to state or condition.

Exercise 15.3   Practice WHO . . . LOOK LIKE, WHAT . . .
                 LIKE, and HOW.

Examples: Teacher   Student

Thomas is sick.   HOW is Thomas?
Jack is intelligent.   WHAT is Jack LIKE?
Bill resembles his father.   WHO does Bill LOOK LIKE?

1. Bob is much better today.
2. Mary resembles her mother.
3. Jim is serious.
4. My son is better today.
5. She has her father's sense of humor.
6. Joe resembles my best friend.
7. He's not very well.
8. She has her mother's eyes and hair.
9. Bob's sister is as attractive as his mother.
10. Snow is cold and white.
11. The weather is hot and humid.

≡ C.1 Observe Linear Measurements.

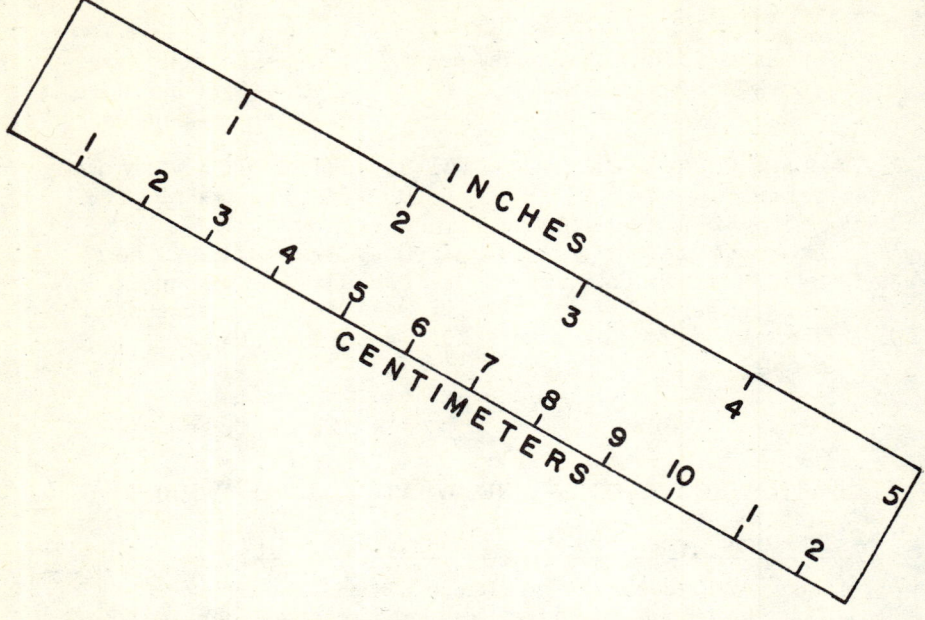

1. How many centimeters is an INCH?	1. An INCH is. . . (2.54 centimeters)
2. What do twelve inches equal?	2. Twelve inches equal . . . (1 FOOT)
3. What do three feet equal?	3. Three feet equal. . .(1 YARD)
4. What do 1760 yards equal?	4. 1760 yards equal. . .(1 MILE)
5. How many inches are there in one foot?	5. There are. . .(twelve inches in one foot)
6. What is the LENGTH of an ordinary ruler?	6. It's. . .(12 inches LONG)
7. What is the WIDTH of a ruler?	7. It's. . .(1 inch WIDE)

Exercise 15.4 Practice LONG and WIDE.

Examples: Teacher   Student

What is the length of the black-   It's about ten feet long.
   board?

What is the width of the black-   It's about three feet wide.
   board?

1. What is the length of your pencil?   6. What is the width of the hall?
2. What is the width of the door?
3. What is the width of this eraser?   7. What is the length of the hall?
4. What is the width of your vocabu-
   lary book?   8. What is the width of the windows?
5. What is the length of this piece of
   chalk?

☰ C.2a Observe Dimensions.

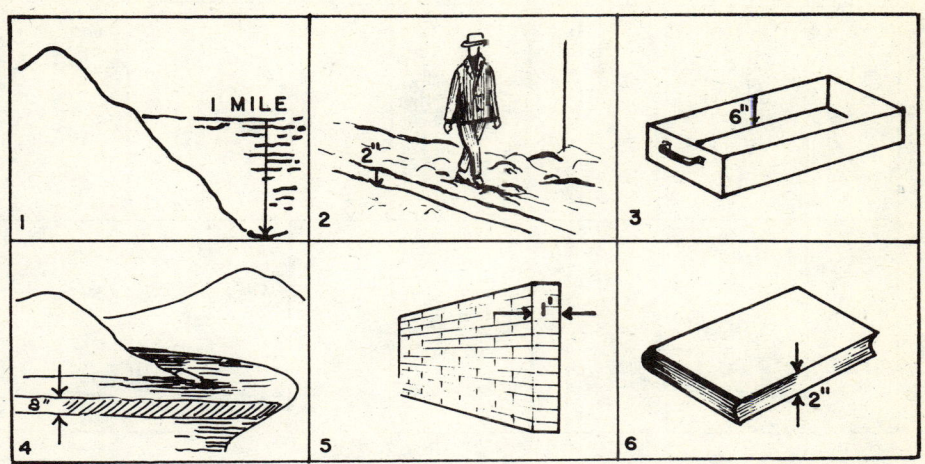

1. What is the DEPTH of the ocean?	1. It's . . . (1 mile DEEP)
2. What is the depth of the snow?	2. It's . . . (2 inches DEEP)
3. What is the depth of the drawer?	3. It's . . . (6 inches DEEP)
4. What is the THICKNESS of the ice?	4. It's . . . (8 inches THICK)
5. What is the thickness of the wall?	5. It's . . . (1 foot THICK)
6. What is the thickness of the book?	6. It's . . . (2 inches THICK)

NOTES: DEEP refers to the distance down from the surface.
          THICK refers to the distance between two surfaces.

Exercise 15.5 Practice DEEP and THICK.

Examples: Teacher   Student

          1 mile, the ocean   The ocean is 1 mile deep.
          8 inches, the ice   The ice is 8 inches thick.

1. 1 foot, the snow   6. 500 feet, Lake Michigan
2. 8 feet, the river   7. 1 inch, the grammar book
3. 10 inches, the wall   8. 2½ feet, the snow
4. 5 inches, the drawer   9. 2 inches, the eraser
5. 3 inches, the book   10. 7 inches, the hole

Exercise 15.6 Practice describing objects.

Example: Teacher   Student

          the dictionary   The dictionary is 9 inches long,
                                  6 inches wide, and 1 inch thick.

1. the pronunciation book   5. a bathtub
2. the drawer in Picture 3   6. a notebook
3. the desk top   7. a wash basin
4. the book in Picture 6   8. a river

☰ C.2b Observe Dimensions.

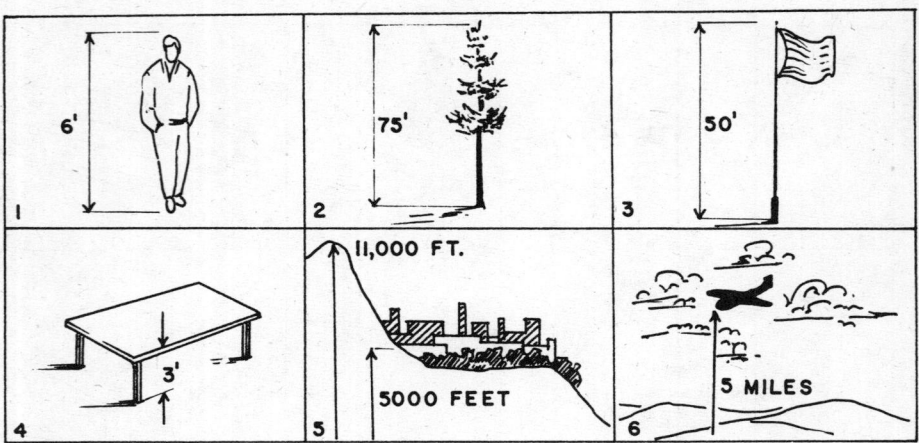

1. What is John's HEIGHT?	1. He's . . . (6 feet TALL)
2. What is the height of the tree?	2. It's . . . (75 feet tall)
3. What is the height of the flagpole?	3. It's . . . (50 feet tall)
4. What is the height of the table?	4. It's . . . (3 feet HIGH)
5. What is the ELEVATION of Denver?	5. It's . . . (5,000 feet high)
6. What is the ALTITUDE of the plane?	6. It's . . . (5 miles high)

NOTES: TALL describes the vertical measurement of people and
"slender" things.
HIGH describes a vertical distance, elevation, or altitude.

Exercise 15.7 Practice TALL and HIGH.

Examples: Teacher   Student

        5 feet 5 inches, Jane   Jane is 5 feet 5 inches tall.
        1 mile, the plane   The plane is 1 mile high.

1. 5 feet 9 inches, John
2. 2 miles, the clouds
3. 55 feet, the flagpole
4. about 29,000 feet, Mt.
   Everest
5. 75 feet, the pine tree

6. 8 feet, the light
7. 25 miles, the jet
8. 2 miles, the mountains
9. 1472 feet, the Empire State
   Building
10. 20 feet, telephone wires

≡ C.3 Observe Weights.

1. How many grams is one OUNCE (1 oz.)?	1. One OUNCE is . . . (28.35 grams)
2. What do sixteen ounces equal?	2. Sixteen ounces equal . . . (1 POUND)
3. What do 2000 pounds (lbs.) equal?	3. 2000 pounds equal. . .(1 TON)
4. What is the WEIGHT of a letter?	4. It weighs . . . (1 ounce)
5. What is the weight of an average man?	5. He weighs . . . (about 155) pounds
6. What is the weight of a car?	6. It weighs . . . (about 1 ton)

Exercise 15.8 Practice Weights.

    Example: Teacher   Student

        What is your weight, Mr. A?   I weigh 145 pounds.

1. What is your weight, Mr. B?
2. What is the weight of your book?
3. What is the weight of a car?

4. What is the weight of sixteen letters? (one ounce each)
5. What is the weight of a baby?
6. What is the weight of all of your books?

≡ C.4 Observe Liquid Measures.

1. How many liters is one PINT?	1. One PINT is . . . (.47 liters)
2. What do two pints equal?	2. Two pints equal . . . (1 QUART)
3. What do four quarts equal?	3. Four quarts equal . . . (1 GALLON)
4. How much milk does an average glass hold?	4. An average glass holds . . . (about 1/2 pint of milk)
5. How much milk should a child drink every day?	5. He should drink . . . (about a quart of milk every day)
6. How much gasoline does a car hold?	6. A car holds . . . (about 18 gallons of gasoline)

Exercise 15.9 Practice Liquid Measures.

Example: <u>Teacher</u>   <u>Student</u>

How much milk do you drink   I drink about a quart of milk
every day?   every day.

1. How much water do you drink every day?
2. How much coffee do you drink every day?
3. How much ice cream do you eat every week?
4. How much milk do you drink every week?
5. How much water do you drink every week?
6. How much milk do you drink every month?
7. How much milk and water do you drink every year?

Review questions.

1. What is the weather like?
2. Who does Mary look like?
3. Does it look like rain today?
4. Does the sky look cloudy?
5. What's your girl friend like?
6. How is your family?
7. Describe your vocabulary book.
8. What is the depth of the ocean?
9. How thick does ice sometimes get?
10. What's your height?
11. How high is this table?

Lesson XVI

A. David West Goes to the Doctor, FEEL.
B. CATCH, HAS; ACHE, SORE.
C. BEFORE, DURING, AFTER.
D. GET IN/OUT OF, GET ON/OFF.

☰ A.   David West Goes to the Doctor.

David usually has to get up at seven in order to get to his eight o'clock class on time. One morning last week he got up at the usual time, but he had a headache and he was sneezing. His roommate said, "You don't look well. Do you feel sick?"

"Yes. I feel terrible. I think I have a cold." He coughed several times.

"Well," his roommate said, "I think you ought to see Dr. Bowman after breakfast. He's a very prominent physician. His office is at 134 Hill Street."

David went to Dr. Bowman's office after his eight o'clock class. When he got there, he saw a beautiful nurse at the desk.

"Would you like to see the doctor?" she asked.

"Yes, please."

"I'm sorry, he's busy right now. May I have your name?"

"David West. May I have your name, too?"

The nurse looked at him angrily. "The doctor will see you in a few minutes," she said. "Please be seated."

David sat down and looked at a magazine for about fifteen minutes. Then a patient came out of the doctor's office, and the nurse told David to go in.

"What seems to be your trouble?" the doctor asked.

"My nose is running, my throat is sore, and my head aches. I'd like to go to the hospital," David answered.

The doctor examined his new patient. "Fortunately, you won't have to go to the hospital," he said. "You have a bad cold, but it's not serious. I'll give you some nose drops, some medicine for your throat, and some aspirin. Follow the directions on the bottle and drink lots of water. You'll feel much better tomorrow."

"Thank you, Dr. Bowman. How much do I owe you?"

"You can pay the nurse when you go out, or ask her to send you a bill."

Exercise 16.1   Practice FEEL.

Examples: Teacher   Student

        sick   A. Do you feel sick?
          fine   B. No, I feel fine.

        worse   C. Do you feel worse?
          better   D. No, I feel better.

1.	well sick	6.	worse better	11.	disagreeable agreeable
2.	very well very sick	7.	very sick very well	12.	tired rested
3.	better worse	8.	sick well	13.	bored interested
4.	much better much worse	9.	gloomy cheerful	14.	displeased pleased
5.	much worse much better	10.	unhappy happy		

≡ B.1   Observe CATCH/CAUGHT and HAS/HAVE/HAD.

David CATCHES a cold   He HAS a cold every winter.
   every winter.

Mary caught the flu last spring.   She had the flu last spring.

John caught pneumonia   He had pneumonia last
   last summer.   summer.

                    He HAD a sore throat yesterday.
                    She had a broken arm last month.
                    John had a headache this morning.

NOTES: Use CATCH for communicable diseases.
         Use HAVE   for both communicable diseases and physical
        abnormalities.

Exercise 16.2   Make sentences with CAUGHT or HAD. (Use
                CAUGHT as much as possible.)

Examples: Teacher   Student

      a cold   David West caught a cold.
      a broken arm   He didn't have a broken arm.

1.	a bad cold	6.	a broken leg
2.	a sore throat	7.	tuberculosis
3.	the flu	8.	a headache
4.	a sprained ankle	9.	small pox
5.	the measles	10.	pneumonia

☰ B.2   Observe ACHE and SORE.

> John: How are you, Mary?
>
> Mary: My head ACHES a little, but otherwise I feel fine. Why are
> you limping, John?
>
> John: I have a SORE ankle. I fell down the stairs last night. By
> the way, Mary, have you seen Jim today?
>
> Mary: No. He told me yesterday that he had a TOOTHACHE and
> that he might have to go to the dentist.

NOTE: SORE often indicates a painful place where the skin is
broken or bruised. ACHE may be internal (an earache);
SORE may be external (a sore ear).

Exercise 16.3   Practice ACHE and SORE.

   a. Examples: <u>Teacher</u>   Student

toothache	A. Jim's tooth aches.
	B. He has a toothache.
earache	C. Bill's ear aches.
	D. He has an earache.

1. toothache	4. backache
2. headache	5. earache
3. stomach-ache	

   b. John has a sore <u>ankle</u>.[1] (Point to parts of body.)

. . . . . foot	. . . . . throat
. . . . . knee	. . . . . elbow
. . . . . shoulder	. . . . leg
. . . . . chest	. . . . . arm
. . . . . hand	. . . . . neck

   c. Use ACHE as much as possible.

      Examples: <u>Teacher</u>   Student

foot	He has a sore foot.
back	He has a backache.

1. elbow	5. ear	9. stomach
2. tooth	6. shoulder	10. finger
3. hand	7. knee	11. back
4. leg	8. head	12. neck

NOTE TO TEACHER: [1]This exercise introduces a type of drill that
will be used extensively in Lessons 16-19. The student should first repeat the key sentence after the teacher ("John has a sore ankle"). Next,
the teacher provides a word or expression ("foot") for the student to
substitute in the key sentence ("John has a sore foot"). Continue with
further substitutions in the same way.

≡ C.   Observe DURING, BEFORE, AFTER.

Situation: Jim and Bill are roommates. Bill is sitting at the desk
when Jim enters their room.

Jim: Did you find your pictures? I put them on your dresser.
Bill: Yes, thanks. I looked at them DURING dinner.

Jim: Are you ready to go to the concert?
Bill: No, not yet. I've got to shower and shave BEFORE we go.

Jim: All right. I'll finish my homework while you do that.
Bill: That reminds me. I'll have to do mine AFTER we come back.

Exercise 16.4   Practice BEFORE, DURING, AFTER.

Examples:	Teacher	Student
	have got to take a shower—go to the concert	I've got to take a shower before I go to the concert.
	looked at my pictures—dinner	I looked at my pictures during dinner.
	hung up my coat—took it off	I hung up my coat after I took it off.

1. took a walk—went to bed	7. studied for the exam—took it
2. visited friends—vacation	8. stayed in my room—storm
3. called her up—gave me her phone number	9. dried my hands—washed them
4. went to school—got dressed	10. ate breakfast—got up
5. had breakfast—came to class	11. tried on the coat—bought it
6. studied—evening	12. picked up the book—dropped it
	13. mailed the letter—wrote it

≡ D.   Observe GET IN/OUT OF and GET ON/OFF.

(Please look at the pictures.)

Teacher	Student
1. What is Mary doing in picture 1?	1. She's . . . (GETTING IN a car)
2. What's she doing in picture 2?	2. She's . . . (GETTING OUT OF a taxi)
3. What's she doing in picture 3?	3. She's . . . (GETTING ON a train)
4. In picture 4?	4. She's . . . (GETTING OFF a bus)
5. What will she do in picture 5?	5. She'll . . . (get on a horse)
6. What will she do in picture 6?	6. She'll . . . (get on a bicycle)
7. In picture 7?	7. She'll . . . (get on a plane)
8. In picture 8?	8. She'll . . . (get on a boat)

NOTES: Use GET IN/OUT OF for small vehicles (cars, taxis, etc.).
          Use GET ON/OFF for large vehicles, two-wheeled vehicles, animals.

Exercise 16.5   Practice GET IN/OUT OF and GET ON/OFF.

Examples: Teacher   Student

    What did Mary do?
       picture 2   She got out of a taxi.
       pictures 5 and 1   She got off a horse and got in a car.

1. picture 4	6. pictures 2 and 8
2. picture 3	7. pictures 5 and 1
3. pictures 2 and 3	8. pictures 6 and 3
4. pictures 4 and 1	9. pictures 6 and 5
5. pictures 4 and 7	10. pictures 7 and 8

Exercise 16.6   Practice GET IN/OUT OF and GET ON/OFF.

1. I got in the car that stopped.[1]
2. (leave)
3. (enter), boat
4. taxi
5. (leave)
6. stopped at the station

7. (enter), train

8. (leave)

9. (enter), limousine

10. was going to the airport

11. bus

12. was waiting
13. streetcar

14. horse

1. I got in the car that stopped.
2. I got out of the car that stopped.
3. I got on the boat that stopped.
4. I got in the taxi that stopped.
5. I got out of the taxi that stopped.
6. I got out of the taxi that stopped at the station.
7. I got on the train that stopped at the station.
8. I got off the train that stopped at the station.
9. I got in the limousine that stopped at the station.
10. I got in the limousine that was going to the airport.
11. I got on the bus that was going to the airport.
12. I got on the bus that was waiting.
13. I got on the streetcar that was waiting.
14. I got on the horse that was waiting.

Summary Dialogue.

Jack: Dr. Brown, I have a sore throat and a headache.
Dr. Brown: (He examines Jack.) You only have a cold. I'll give you a prescription for some medicine.
Jack: Thank you. Shall I come back tomorrow?
Dr. Brown: No, come back next week instead.

Comprehension questions for Part A, "David West Goes to the Doctor." (For classroom use or homework.)

1. How did David West feel?
2. What did his roommate ask him?
3. What did David say?
4. Who is Dr. Bowman?
5. Did David go to see him after breakfast?
6. What did Dr. Bowman's nurse say to David? What else?
7. Do you think she was very angry?
8. How long did David have to wait?
9. What did he do while he was waiting?
10. What did David tell the doctor?
11. What did Dr. Bowman say?
12. What kind of medicine did he give David?
13. How does the story end?

NOTE TO TEACHER: [1] Underlining indicates those parts of the key sentence that will be varied by means of substitution items.

Review questions.

1. How do you feel?
2. Why did your friend go to the dentist?
3. Why did David West go to the doctor? (Use: SORE)
4. Do you hang up your coat before you take it off?
5. Do you usually write letters after you mail them?
6. What did you do during the weekend?
7. Do you sometimes get on a taxi and go to town?
8. When was the last time that you got off your car?

Lesson XVII

A. Parties, INVITE.
B. HOLD, KEEP.
C. GUESS, WONDER, FIND OUT.
D. GET ALONG, GET THROUGH (WITH).
E. JUST.

≡ A.1   Parties.

Situation: John is talking with his new friend, Tom.

> John: When did you come to Springfield, Tom?
> Tom: We moved here last week.
> John: Do you know any girls yet?
> Tom: No, I don't. Why?
> John: We're having a party at my house this Saturday and I'd like to invite you. Would you go on a blind date?
> Tom: I'd rather not. The last one I went on wasn't very pleasant.
> John: All right. I know, I'll introduce you to my girl friend's sister.

≡ A.2   Observe INVITE.

Situation: Tom is talking with John after the party.

> Tom: John, thanks for INVITING me to your party. I had a very good time.
> John: I'm glad you were able to come, Tom. I thought it was an excellent party.
> Tom: So did I. Mary introduced me to several girls.
>
> John: Why don't you invite somebody to the student program next Friday?
> Tom: That's a good idea. I think I'll ask Mary.

Exercise 17.1   Practice the dialogue until the students know it well.

Exercise 17.2   Practice the following sentences.[1]

a. Thanks for
          inviting <u>me</u> <u>to your party</u>.
              . . . them to the movies
              . . . . her to go to the concert
              . . . . him to go to Detroit
              . . . . him to go to your country
              . . . . . me to come to your house
              . . . them to come to dinner
              . . . . her to dinner
              . . . . . us for dinner

b. I thought
          <u>the party</u> was very pleasant.
      . . the dance . . . .
      . . my date . . . . .
      . . the blind date . . . .
      . . the picnic . . . .

c. I had
          <u>a very good</u> time.
      . . . a wonderful . . . .
      . . . an excellent . . . .
      . . . an enjoyable . . . .
      . . . a very enjoyable . .

d. Mary introduced me to <u>several girls</u>.
              . . . her mother and father
              . . . her brother
              . . . the hostess
              . . . the host
              . . . many people
              . . . several of her friends
              . . . all of her friends

e. Why don't you
          invite <u>someone to the program</u>?
              . . . one of your friends to
                    the party
              . . . somebody to the picnic
              . . . your girl friend to the
                    concert
              . . . one of your friends to
                    the dance
              . . . your girl friend to the
                    dance
              . . . your friends to the
                    program

f. I think
          I'll <u>ask Mary</u>.
      . . . make a date with . .
      . . . ask . . . . .
      . . . make a date with . .
      . . . invite . . . .
      . . . ask . . . . .
      . . . ask . . . . . (them)

NOTE TO TEACHER: [1] These exercises can be done one at a time or in pairs; for example, one-half of the students can give the question in 17.2e and the other half, the answer in 17.2f. The teacher supplies the cue for each new response.

Dots indicate those parts of the preceding sentence that are to be repeated.

☰ B.1   Observe HOLD.

Teacher	Student
What am I holding?	You're holding a book.
What am I holding now?	You're holding a pen.
(Please look at the pictures.)	
1. What's Joe doing in picture 1?	1. He's . . . (HOLDING some packages)
2. What's he doing in picture 2?	2. He's . . . (HOLDING her COAT for her)
3. What's he doing in picture 3?	3. He's . . . (HOLDING her CHAIR for her)
4. What's he doing in picture 4?	4. He's . . . (HOLDING the DOOR for her)

Exercise 17.3   Practice HOLD.

Joe held the packages while she looked for her key.
. . . . unlocked the door
. . . . her coat . . . .
. . . . put it on
. . . . sat down
. . . her chair   . . . .
. . . the chair   . . . .
. . . . .   for her to sit in
. . . . .   for her
. . . . the coat . . . . .
. . . . the door . . . . .
. . . the car door . . . . .
. . . . .   while she got in
. . . . .   while she got out

☰ B.2   Observe KEEP.

Teacher	Student
Where do I keep my pen?	You keep it in your pocket.
Where do you keep your watch?	I keep it on my wrist.
(Please look at the pictures.)	
1. What does the man in picture 1 do with his money?	1. He . . . (KEEPS it in a bank)
2. What does he do with his clothes?	2. He . . . (keeps them in a closet)
3. What does he do with his car?	3. He . . . (keeps it in a garage)
4. What does he do with his dishes?	4. He . . . (keeps them in a cupboard)

Exercise 17.4   Practice KEEP.

Examples: Teacher   Student

money in the bank — room   You should keep your money in the bank instead of in your room.

car in the garage -- in front of your house   You should keep your car in the garage instead of in front of your house.

1. money in the bank — room
2. best clothes in the closet —suitcase
3. books in the bookcase -- floor
4. new car in the garage — yard

5. money in the bank-- drawer
6. dishes in the cupboard -- sink
7. feet on the floor -- desk

≡ C.1   Observe GUESS.

Situation: Joe and Jane are talking.

> Joe: Do you have any brothers or sisters?
> Jane: Yes. GUESS how many I have.
>
> Joe: Two brothers?
> Jane: No, guess again.
>
> Joe: One brother and two sisters?
> Jane: No.
>
> Joe: I can't guess.
> Jane: I have four brothers and three sisters.

Exercise 17.5   Practice GUESS.

a. Guess how many <u>brothers and sisters</u> <u>I have.</u>
   . . . . brothers . . . . .
   . . . . sisters . . . . . .
   . . . . children . . . . .
   . . . . I know
   . . . . languages . . . .
   . . . . I speak

b. Examples: <u>Teacher</u>   <u>Student</u>

who I am   A. Can you guess who I am?
                    B. No, I can't guess who you are.

where I'm from   C. Can you guess where I'm from?
                    D. No, I can't guess where you're
                       from.

1. what country I'm from   6. where I live
2. what city I'm from   7. why I came to this country
3. what language I speak   8. how I got here
4. what I'm studying   9. who my girl friend is
5. what my name is   10. what my sister's name is

≡ C.2   Observe WONDER.

Situation: Pari, who is from Iran, and Rosa, who is from Spain, see
            some strange animals while they are walking to school.

Pari: Look, Rosa! I WONDER what that is. Do you know?
Rosa: No, I don't. There's another one in the tree.

Pari: I wonder what they are.
Rosa: Let's ask our teacher when we get to school.

Pari: (At school.) Mr. Gray, we saw some strange animals while we
        were walking to school, and we are wondering what they
        were.

Mr. Gray: What did they look like?
Pari: They were small and brown.
Mr. Gray: Were they furry animals? Did they have long bushy tails?
Pari: Yes.
Mr. Gray: Then, your question is easy to answer. You saw some
            squirrels. There are a lot of them in this city.

Exercise 17.6   Practice WONDER.

I wonder what that is.
. . . .where it went
. . . .   John . . .
. . . . .who he is
. . . .   that woman is
. . . .   those people are
. . . . .what they're doing
. . . .   he's doing
. . . .   his sister did yesterday
. . . .   Mary's eating
. . . .   Bill's thinking
. . . .   he's studying
. . . .where Jack went
. . . . .when . . . .
. . . .   Bill arrived here
. . . .   Bill got here
. . . . .how Dave feels
. . . . is
. . how tall . . . . . .
. . . . . .old . . . . . .
. . . .   his brother is

≡ C.3   Observe FIND OUT.

Situation: Marie and Henry are in their new apartment. A strange noise woke them up early this morning. They think it was a burglar.

Marie: Did you FIND OUT what that noise was?
Henry: No. I asked several people, but nobody else heard it.

Marie: We ought to find out what it was.
Henry: I'll try again.

(Henry goes out. Three hours later he comes back.)

Henry: Marie, I found out what the noise was.
Marie: Good. I heard it again a couple of minutes ago.

Henry: (Laughing.) I know. It's a squirrel. It jumps from a tree to the roof of the house. Then it runs back and forth across the roof.

Exercise 17.7   Practice FIND OUT.

He found out what it was.
. . . . where . . . . .
. . . . went
. . . . . what it did
. . . . they did
. . . how much . . . . . .
. . . . studied
. . . . knew
. . . . . little . . . . . .
. . . . walked
. . . . slowly . . . .
. . . . . long . . . .
. . . . the English course was
. . . . it was
. . . . . when . . . . .
. . . . it started
. . . . . . ended

≡ D.   Observe GET ALONG, GET THROUGH (WITH).

Situation: Bill and Jane got up late this morning. They are eating breakfast.

Bill: Do your sister and her husband GET ALONG well together?
Jane: Yes, they are very happy. They never quarrel.

Bill: What time will the children GET THROUGH WITH their lessons today?
Jane: They finish at three o'clock.

Bill: Excuse me, I didn't hear what you said.
Jane: I said that they'll GET THROUGH at three.

Exercise 17.8   Practice GET ALONG and GET THROUGH (WITH).

Examples:	Teacher	Student

Sue finished her work.   She got through with her work.
Sue finished at three.   She got through at three.
Sue and Joe are good friends.   They get along well together.

1. Joan finished her homework.
2. Bob and his girl friend always quarrel.
3. Jack finished at eight o'clock.
4. The men finish work at four-thirty.
5. The two girls are very good friends.

6. The students finished the course yesterday.
7. Bill and Jane never quarrel.
8. Tom and John are always arguing.
9. He finished the assignment by noon.
10. We finished at 11:30.

≡ E.   Observe JUST.

Situation: James and Henry run into each other on the campus.

James: Hello, Henry. Did you remember your appointment with Professor Black?
Henry: Yes, I did, James. I JUST came from his office.

James: JUST NOW?
Henry: Yes, just now. I left him exactly three minutes ago.

NOTE: JUST means *recently*. (Other uses of JUST are taught in Lesson 18.)

Exercise 17.9   Practice JUST with simple past.

Examples:	Teacher	Student

finish his assignment   Dan just finished his assignment.
go to the store   Dan just went to the store.
eat his dinner   Dan just ate his dinner.

1. come back from the program
2. begin his homework
3. buy a new car
4. receive some money from home
5. write to his sister

6. ask Susan for a date
7. make a long distance call
8. finish his homework
9. get through with his work
10. talk with Mary

Review questions.

1. What am I holding?
2. What do you hold for a woman to sit in?
3. Where do you keep your money?

4. Where do you keep your clothes?
5. Who did you invite to the program?
6. What do you like to guess?
7. What do you often wonder about?
8. What did you find out yesterday?

Lesson XVIII

A. Telephone Calls.
B. SOMEWHERE, EVERYWHERE, ANYWHERE, etc.
C. JUST.

≡ A.1   Long-distance phone calls.

Situation: Sam Drake wants to place a station-to-station
call to his friend Bill in Miami, Florida.

> (Sam deposits a dime in a pay telephone and dials ''0''
> for Operator.)
>
> Operator: Operator.
> Sam: I'd like to place a call to Miami, Florida. The
> number is LI 7-4316.
>
> Operator: One moment please.
> Dial 1 for long distance, 305 for Miami area
> code, and then the number you want. Would
> you like me to place the call for you?
> Sam: If you would, please.
>
> (The operator returns Sam's dime, and dials
> 1-305-LI 7-4316.)
>
> Operator: What number are you calling from?
> Sam: 669-7654 (Number of pay phone).
>
> (Bill answers the phone in Miami.)
>
> Operator: (To Sam.) Deposit seventy-five cents for the
> first three minutes, please.

≡ A.2   Campus phone calls.

> Situation: Tom and his girl friend Mary plan to go bowling
> at ten p.m., after they have done their home-
> work. Tom dials Mary's dormitory number.

Operator: North Hall.
Tom: I'd like extension 704 please.
Operator: Just a moment. I'll ring it for you.

Mary: Hello. Mary Brown speaking.
Tom: Hello, Mary. This is Tom. It's only 8:45, but
I've already finished my homework assign-
ments. Have you finished yet?

Mary: No, I'm still working on my algebra. The problems are very difficult.
Tom: Can't your roommate help you?

Mary: I don't have a roommate any more. Do you
think you could explain the problems to me?
Tom: I'll be happy to. Do you want me to come over there?

Mary: No, I've got a better idea. Let's go bowling now
and do the problems afterwards.
Tom: Whatever you say. I'll pick you up in ten minutes.

Exercise 18.1   Practice the following sentences.

a.   It's only eight but I've already finished my homework.
. . . we've . . . . . . arrived at the station
. . . our relatives have . . . . . . arrived
. . . John has . . . . . . gone home
. . . . the program has . . . . . . begun
. . . they have . . . . . . begun to sing

b. It was only eight but they had already begun to sing.
. . . . begun to argue
. . . . . the program had . . . . . . begun
. . . . they had . . . . . . arrived
. . . . . he was . . . . . . tired of waiting
. . . . she was . . . . . . impatient

c.   Student A   Student B

Have you finished yet?   No, I'm still working on my algebra.
Have you found it . . .   . . . looking for it
Has she arrived . . .   . . . waiting for her
Are they here . . .   . . . waiting for them
Hasn't he arrived . . .   . . . waiting for him
Are you ready . . .   . . . combing my hair
Isn't my car ready . . .   . . . we're . . . working on it
Has the sun come out . . .   . it's . . . behind the clouds
Have they left . . .   . . they're . . . here

d.   I don't <u>have a roommate</u> any more.
                    . . . . live there . . . .
                    . . . .work there . . . .
                    . . . . . .like her . . . .
                    . . . . visit them . . . .
                    . . . . . call on Helen . . . .
        He's not reading the paper . . . .
                    . . . studying English . . . .
                    . . . . . . .living here . . . .
                    . . . . . .staying here . . . .

e.   I'll <u>pick you up</u> <u>in ten minutes.</u>
                    . . . . . at seven-thirty
        . . call for you . . . . . .
                    . . . . . at seven tonight
        . . . .meet you . . . . . .
                    . . . . . at the bowling alley
                    . . . . . at the skating rink
                    . . . . . at the stadium
                    . . . . . at the theater
        . .wait for you . . . . . .
        . .look for you . . . . . .

≡ B.1   Observe SOMEWHERE, SOMEBODY, SOMETIME.

        Situation: Virginia and Martha are talking about their
                    friend Mary.

Virginia: Where's Mary?
Martha: She's SOMEWHERE in Europe.
Virginia: Do you know where?
Martha: No, I don't. SOMEBODY thought she might be
in Holland.
Virginia: When did you hear that?
Martha: I don't remember for sure. I think it was
SOMETIME last week.

        NOTE: Use SOME- for an unspecified place, time, per-
               son, or thing.

        Exercise 18.2   Practice SOMEWHERE, SOMEBODY, SOMETIME.

        Examples: <u>Teacher</u>   <u>Student</u>

        He built a house in the city.   He built a house somewhere
          I don't know exactly where.   in the city.
        A man is looking for you.   Somebody is looking for you.
          I don't know who he is.

1. We're going to have an election in November. I don't know exactly when.
2. His house is near here. I don't know exactly where.
3. I'm going to France next year. I don't know exactly when.
4. The meeting is on Thursday. I don't know exactly when.
5. The Campus Theater is near here. I don't know exactly where.
6. A man is waiting for you. I don't know who he is.
7. School ends in May. I don't know exactly when.
8. He lives in the United States. I don't know exactly where.
9. He received your letter last month. I don't know exactly when.
10. A lady is waiting to see you. I don't know who she is.

≡ B.2   Observe EVERYBODY, EVERYTHING, EVERYWHERE.

Situation: The students are in biology class. They are planning to study a frog.

Mr. Black:	Is EVERYBODY here today?
Class:	No, one person is absent.
Mr. Black:	Did you bring EVERYTHING we need?
Class:	We brought all the things you asked for.
Mr. Black:	Did you bring the frog, James?
James:	I'm sorry, Mr. Black; I couldn't find a frog. I looked EVERYWHERE—in the park, along the river, by the lake; but I couldn't find a single one.
Mr. Black:	That's all right. I have one in my office.

NOTE: Use EVERY- to express ALL PEOPLE, ALL THINGS, ALL PLACES.

Exercise 18.3   Practice EVERYBODY, EVERYTHING, EVERYWHERE.

Examples: Teacher	Student
Has he phoned all the people?	Yes, he's phoned everybody.
Have they put all the things in the car?	Yes, they've put everything in the car.
Have you gone to many places?	Yes, we've gone everywhere.

1. Has the entire class arrived?
2. Have you met all the students?
3. Have you bought all your school supplies?
4. Have all your things arrived from your country?
5. Have all your friends come this evening?
6. Have they looked in all the rooms for the watch?
7. Have you traveled to many countries?
8. Has she brought all the things we need?
9. Have all the people left for the concert?

☰ B.3   Observe ANYTHING, ANYWHERE, etc.; NOTHING, NOWHERE, etc.

Situation: Robert and his wife, Betty, are making plans for the evening.

Robert: What would you like to do tonight, Betty?
Betty: ANYTHING you like. What do you want to do?
Robert: NOTHING in particular.
Betty: Then let's stay home and watch television.

Robert: Is there ANYBODY we should visit?
Betty: NOBODY I can think of.

Robert: Then why don't we go somewhere? ANYWHERE; you decide.
Betty: No, NOWHERE. I prefer to stay home and relax tonight.

NOTE: Use ANY- to express *it makes no difference.*
       NOTHING, NOWHERE, etc. express NOT
       ANYTHING, NOT ANYWHERE, etc.

Exercise 18.4   Practice ANYTHING, ANYBODY, etc.

Examples: Teacher   Student

What shall we do tonight?   Anything you like.
Should I ask Sue for a date?   You can ask anybody you like.
When shall I pick you up?   Anytime you like.

1. Who shall we ask for dinner?   6. Should we meet at the library?
2. What might we do this evening?   7. Should I tell you my plans?
3. When may I call you up?   8. Can I go to Europe by plane?
4. How should we go to Europe?   9. May I call you up at seven tonight?
5. Where can I buy some clothes?   10. Shall we ask the Browns to
                                         dinner?

☰ C.1   Observe JUST.

Situation: Roger is talking with Mr. White at the dormitory.

Roger: Are you a teacher, Mr. White?
Mr. White: Not now. I taught school last year, but now I'm
            JUST a student.

Roger: Do you live here?
Mr. White: No, I just eat here. I live on Ann Street.

NOTE: JUST means *only, nothing more than.*

Exercise 18.5   Practice JUST meaning *only.*

Examples: Teacher   Student

Are you a teacher?   No, I'm just a student.
Do you have a quarter?   No, I just have a dime.

1. Are you a teacher, Mr. A?
2. Do you have a pencil, Mr. B?
3. Do you have $5.00?
4. Do you have five books?
5. Did you bring your grammar book?
6. Do you have eleven fingers?
7. Do you have six classes?
8. Did Bob have $5.00?
9. Did you meet Jack and Sue?
10. Do you speak German?

≡ C.2   Observe JUST.

Situation: Robert is eating dinner with Dr. Brown.

> Robert: Are you a student here too, Dr. Brown?
> Dr. Brown: Yes. Now I'm a student JUST like you.
>
> Robert: How do you like the soup?
> Dr. Brown: It's just right. I like soup that's neither too
>   hot nor too cold.

NOTE: JUST[1] means *exactly*.

Exercise 18.6   Practice JUST meaning *exactly*.

John <u>looks</u> just like <u>me</u>.
. . . . his father
. . . . just the same as . . . .
. . . . talks . . . .
. . . . his brother
. . . writes . . . .
. . . . just about like . . . . .
. . . . just as bad as . . . . .
. . . . just as good as . . . .
. . . . just like . . . .

Summary Dialogue.

Jack: Are you going to Detroit for the weekend?
Joe: No, I'm just going for one day. I'm not going anywhere Sunday.

Jack: Someone called you just before you came in. I think it was your
      girl friend.
Joe: I expected a call from her. I saw her with my best friend just
      about an hour ago.

Review questions.

1. Where's Mary Smith now? (Use: SOME)
2. Have you met all the students here?
3. What had the students brought for the experiment?
4. Where have you been traveling?
5. What would you like to do tonight?
6. Where would you like to go?
7. Who would you like to call on next week?

NOTE TO TEACHER: [1]JUST with a number has two possible meanings. For example, "just 10 a.m." may mean "exactly 10 a.m." or "only 10 a.m." The meaning depends on context and intonation.

Lesson XIX

A. COVERED WITH, FILLED WITH, etc.
B. MARRIED TO, USED TO, etc.
C. FULL OF, TIRED OF, etc.
D. FRIGHTENED BY, etc.; SURPRISED AT.
E. Campus Activities.

≡ A.1   Observe COVERED WITH, BORED WITH, PLEASED WITH, DISAPPOINTED WITH.

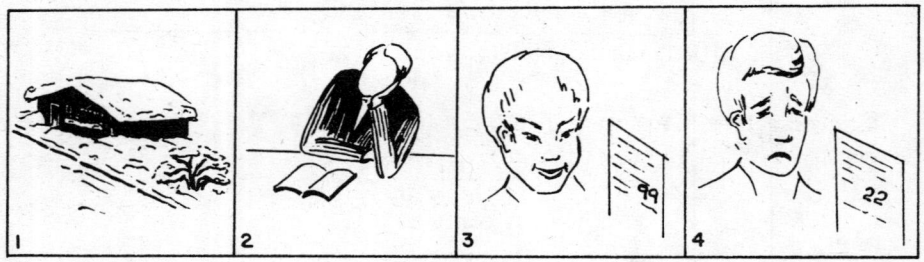

Teacher	Student
1. Describe the house in picture 1.	1. It'S . . . (COVERED WITH snow)
2. Describe the student in picture 2.	2. He'S . . . (BORED WITH his book)
3. Describe the boy in picture 3.	3. He'S . . . (PLEASED WITH his grade)
4. Describe the boy in picture 4.	4. He'S . . . (DISAPPOINTED WITH his grade)

Exercise 19.1   Practice COVERED WITH, etc.

Examples: Teacher   Student

    table—covered   The table is covered with papers.
    Mr. Jones—pleased   Mr. Jones is pleased with the program.
    Susan—bored   Susan is bored with her classes.

1. desk—covered	6. walls—covered
2. Jane--bored	7. actor--pleased
3. road—covered	8. Frank--disappointed
4. Edison—pleased	9. reporter—pleased
5. Mr. Brown—disappointed	10. audience—bored

≡ A.2   Observe FILLED WITH, ACQUAINTED WITH.

Situation: Tom and Bob are roommates at the university.

> Tom: Bob, do you know Helen Smith?
> Bob: No, I'M not ACQUAINTED WITH her.
>
> Tom: That's too bad. Were there many people at the con-
>   cert?
> Bob: Yes. The hall WAS FILLED WITH students.

Exercise 19.2   Practice FILLED WITH and ACQUAINTED WITH.

Examples: <u>Teacher</u>   <u>Student</u>

Do you know Tom?   Yes, I'm acquainted with him.
Were there many stu-   Yes, it was filled with students.
   dents in the concert hall?

1. Do you know Jim?   5. Does Tom know Bob?
2. Does Jim know you?   6. Is there anything in the box?
3. Is there much water in the   7. Are there many books in the
      glass?   library?
4. Are there many people in the   8. Do you know Jane?
      room?

≡ B.   Observe MARRIED TO, USED TO,[1] ACCUSTOMED TO.

Tom IS MARRIED TO Betty.	Tom is Betty's husband.
Sally IS USED TO cooking. Sally IS ACCUSTOMED TO cooking.	Sally has done a lot of cook- ing.
Mary is accustomed to the weather.	The weather doesn't bother her.

Exercise 19.3   Practice MARRIED TO, etc.

Examples: <u>Teacher</u>   <u>Student</u>

married—dentist   She's married to a dentist.
accustomed—working   She's accustomed to working.
used—hot weather   She's used to hot weather.

1. married—professor   7. married—Jim
2. accustomed—weather   8. accustomed—city life
3. used—blind dates   9. used—studying at night
4. married—Tom   10. married—Frank
5. accustomed—walking   11. accustomed—cold winters
6. used—waiting for me   12. used—American food

NOTE TO TEACHER: [1]Note contrast: "She USED TO cook." and
"She IS USED TO cooking."

☰ C.   Observe FULL OF, TIRED OF, AFRAID OF, PROUD OF.

The room IS FULL OF people.	Many people are in the room.
Robert IS TIRED OF school.	School doesn't interest him.
Criminals ARE AFRAID OF police dogs.	Police dogs frighten them.
Mrs. Blue IS PROUD OF her son.	He makes very high grades.

Exercise 19.4   Practice FULL OF, etc.

Examples: <u>Teacher</u>   <u>Student</u>

The closet is full.	It's full of clothes.
The people were proud.	They were proud of their history.
The girl is tired.	She's tired of studying.
The child was afraid.	He was afraid of the dark.

1. The drawer was full.	6. Tommy was tired.
2. The engineer was tired.	7. The theater was full.
3. The bird was afraid.	8. Bobby was afraid.
4. The room was full.	9. Mrs. Green was proud.
5. The man was proud.	10. The students were tired.

☰ D.   Observe AMUSED BY, FRIGHTENED BY, SURROUNDED BY;
        SURPRISED AT.

Situation: Betty and Jane have just arrived at the zoo.

Jane:	I wonder why those people are laughing.
Betty:	I think they'RE AMUSED BY the monkeys.
Jane:	I'd like to see the lions while we're here, but I'M always FRIGHTENED BY their roars.
Betty:	They can't hurt you, Jane. Remember that they'RE SURROUNDED BY a fence.
Jane:	Oh yes, that's true. Betty, did you expect to see so many people here today?
Betty:	No, I'M SURPRISED AT that too. Usually only a few people come here during the afternoon.

Exercise 19.5   Practice FRIGHTENED BY, AMUSED BY, etc.

Examples:	Teacher	Student
	The child cried when the lion roared.	The child was frightened by the lion.
	The people thought the animals were funny.	The people were amused by the animals.
	The thief was in the middle of the policemen.	The thief was surrounded by the policemen.

1. The director had many actors around him.
2. The children thought the animals were funny.
3. They ran when they heard the lion roar.
4. The tourists hadn't expected such a large pyramid.
5. They laughed when they heard the story.
6. The football captain gathered the players around him.
7. The shoppers hadn't expected such stormy weather.
8. She screamed when she saw the criminal.

≡ E.1   Putting on an exhibition.

Situation: Bob Jones is explaining an exhibition.

"The electrical engineering students are putting on this exhibition in order to acquaint the public with some of the progress that has been made with electricity during this century.

"We are displaying many things of historical interest. For example, here are some of the first light bulbs that Edison invented. Next to them are some modern light bulbs. Notice how different they look.

"The development of electricity has made living much easier for many people, especially the housewife. Today housewives use electric stoves, mixers, and toasters to prepare food, and they use electric irons, washing machines, and clothes dryers to do the laundry.

"Finally, electricity has led to the development of radios, phonographs, and television. These three things have made life more enjoyable for everyone."

Exercise 19.6   Comprehension questions.

1. What is an exhibition?
2. Why did the electrical engineering students put on an exhibition?
3. Did they display anything of historical interest?
4. How has the development of electricity made living easier?
5. How has the development of electricity made living more enjoyable?

☰ E.2   Making reservations for a play.

> Situation: Dick and John are interested in a Shakespearean play at the
>   theater. They go to the ticket window to make reserva-
>   tions.

John: It's 9:10 but the agent hasn't come yet.
Dick: He just came in.

John: (To agent.) We'd like to reserve two seats for the Friday evening
         performance of Hamlet.
Agent: I'm sorry. Friday evening is already sold out.

John: Do you have anything for Saturday evening?
Agent: Yes. This seating chart shows you where the seats are.

John: We'd like something down front. Can you give us these seats on
         the inside aisle?
Agent: Yes. Here are your tickets, seats eight and ten in Row B.

Exercise 19.7   Practice the following sentences.

I'd like to reserve two seats.
          . . . . some seats down front
          . . . . on the inside aisle
          . . . . in the balcony
Can you give me . . . .
Do you have . . . .
          . . . . on the plane to Chicago

Summary Dialogue.

Helen: This is an excellent show. We'll have to stand in line until
         some seats are available.

Jane: One of my classmates said she was frightened by the main
         feature but amused by the cartoon.
Helen: Betty told me there was nothing to be afraid of; but she said it
         was full of surprises. I still want to see it.

Jane: Well, at least we won't be bored with it.
Helen: No. I think we'll find it very good. Some of the girls were
         disappointed with the way it ended, but I think we'll enjoy it.

Review questions.

1. Why did you leave the concert before it was over?
2. What's in the cup?
3. Do you know Bob?
4. Why did the woman praise her son?
5. Why did Robert turn the radio off after four hours?
6. Why did the criminal run from the dog?
7. When do people laugh?
8. Why do people run when they hear a lion roar?

Lesson XX

A. Review questions.
B. Review exercises.

A. Review questions. (Each section corresponds to a lesson; A.11 reviews Lesson XI, A.12 reviews Lesson XII, etc.)

A.11
1. What languages can you speak?
2. Where might you go next weekend?
3. What should you do tonight?
4. Which would you rather do, eat or sleep?
5. What shall we do tomorrow?

A.12
1. What did you take off when you got up this morning?
2. What did you put on after you got up this morning?
3. What are you trying to do here?
4. What do you intend to do after this course?
5. What are you going to pass tomorrow?

A.13
1. How long do you usually wait for someone?
2. When do you expect to leave here?
3. Why does a student have to study?
4. What should you be able to do in a few weeks?
5. What would you like to take?

A.14
1. Which season is the most pleasant?
2. Which season is the least pleasant?
3. What did you forget to do yesterday?
4. Who usually reminded you to do things at home?
5. Who does your cousin remind you of?

A.15
1. What was the weather like yesterday?
2. What does your friend look like?
3. Who does your friend look like?
4. What is your friend like?
5. Can you remember the measurements taught in Lesson 15?

A.16
1. What's the matter with your arm?
2. What's wrong with your friend?
3. Do you ever take a walk after you go to bed?
4. How did you get here? (Use: GET ON, etc.)
5. Can you get in a motorcycle or a motor scooter?

A.17
1. Who do you hope to make a date with?
2. What do people usually keep in garages?
3. What should men hold for women?
4. What would you like to find out?
5. Try to guess what he has in his pocket.

A.18
1. What have you got in your pocket?
2. Have you learned anything this week?
3. Had you studied English before this course?
4. How have you been practicing these lessons?
5. Have you learned everything now?

A.19
1. When do people wear snow boots?
2. What was the boy pleased with?
3. When do you usually get bored?
4. What are you surprised at here in the United States?
5. Are you used to American life now?

☰ B. Review exercises.

Exercise 20.1 COUPLE, PAIR.

Examples: <u>Teacher</u>   Student

market   A. Why did you go to the market?
steaks   B. In order to get a couple of steaks.

store   C. Why did you go to the store?
slacks   D. In order to get a pair of slacks.

1. store	3. post office	5. store
gloves	air letters	socks
2. bank	4. drugstore	6. clothing store
check books	magazines	shirts

Exercise 20.2   PASS, SPEND.

Examples: Teacher   Student

$5.00   We spent $5.00 for tickets.
two days   We spent two days at the beach.
the sugar   He passed the sugar.

1. the salt	5. two months abroad	8. the house
2. fifteen dollars	6. twelve dollars for a	9. the napkins
3. two weeks in Florida	license	10. forty dollars
4. the examination	7. the other car	

Exercise 20.3   WAIT, EXPECT, HOPE.

Examples: <u>Teacher</u>   <u>Student</u>

Who are you waiting for?   I'm waiting for my friend.
When do you expect him?   I expect him at four.
Will he be here soon?   I hope he will.

1. Who are you waiting for?   7. Are you going to college this
2. When do you expect him?   fall?
3. Will he be here soon?   8. Will you be here for class to-
4. Are you getting a degree this spring?   morrow?
5. Why are you standing here?   9. Why are you here at the bus
6. Are you learning much English?   station?

Exercise 20.4   TAKE.

Examples: Teacher   Student

a walk   I took a walk.
a cab to the airport   I took a cab to the airport.
a ten-minute break   I took a ten-minute break.
a week to drive there   I took a week to drive there.

1. a job in Cleveland   5. a lot of baggage with me
2. a bus to Detroit   6. a two-week vacation in Florida
3. the English course at the   7. a plane to New York
    Institute   8. a few pictures on my trip
4. a week to drive here

Exercise 20.5   HAVE TO, BE ABLE TO, OUGHT TO.

Examples: <u>Teacher</u>   <u>Student</u>

I must work.   I have to work.
I can speak English.   I am able to speak English.
I should leave at once.   I ought to leave at once.

1. I must take an exam.   6. I can type.
2. I should study harder.   7. I should be more ambitious.
3. I can speak two languages   8. I must speak louder.
     fluently.   9. I can play the piano.
4. I must watch my temper.   10. I should pay this bill.
5. I should stop smoking.

Exercise 20.6   REMEMBER, REMIND.

Examples: <u>Teacher</u>   <u>Student</u>

        my birthday   A. Will you remember my birthday?
                           B. Yes, my friend will remind me.
        call on us   C. Will you remember to call on us?
                           D. Yes, my wife will remind me.

1. the formula   4. his first name   7. my birthday
2. the story   5. to go to the bank   8. to write
3. to go   6. the appointment

Exercise 20.7   REMIND TO do something, REMIND OF something.

Examples: <u>Teacher</u>   <u>Student</u>

He reminded me of the lecture.   He reminded me to go to the lecture.
He reminded me to get the money.   He reminded me of the money.
He reminded me of the rent.   He reminded me to pay the rent.

1. He reminded me to work the   5. He reminded me of my book.
     problem.   6. He reminded me of the exam.
2. He reminded me of the show.   7. He reminded me to borrow some
3. He reminded me of the letter.   money.
4. He reminded me to get my wrist- 8. He reminded me to study the
     watch.   lesson.

Exercise 20.8   LONG, WIDE, DEEP, THICK.

Examples: <u>Teacher</u>   <u>Student</u>

        dictionary   The dictionary is nine inches long,
                            six inches wide, and two inches
                            thick.
        desk drawer   The desk drawer is two feet long, one
                            foot wide, and four inches deep.

1. notebook   4. door   7. finger
2. box   5. desk drawer   8. wash basin
3. grammar book   6. bathtub

Exercise 20.9   HIGH, TALL .

Examples: Teacher   Student

Jack, 6 ft.—John, 5 ft. 10 in.   Jack is taller than John.
airplane, 1 mi.—the trees, 75 ft.   The airplane is higher than the trees.

1. Mary, 5 ft. 6 in.—Sue, 5 ft. 3 in.   5. clouds, 25 mi.—jet plane,
2. clouds, 1 mi.—mountain, 2500 ft.   2 mi.
3. pine tree, 80 ft.—telephone pole,   6. flag pole—Jack
   12 ft.   7. ceiling—doorknob
4. Jim, 6 ft.—Bob, 5 ft. 11 in.   8. blackboard—floor

Exercise 20.10   WHAT . . . LIKE, HOW.

Examples: Teacher   Student

        Mary is friendly and pretty.   What is Mary like?
        Mr. Smith is very well.   How is Mr. Smith?
        Snow is cold and white.   What is snow like?

1. Bob is intelligent.   5. Mary is over her illness.
2. Mr. Brown is feeling better.   6. I'm fine.
3. My brother has recovered.   7. Jim is tall and serious.
4. The house is large and square.

Exercise 20.11   LOOK and LOOK LIKE with AND.

Examples: Teacher   Student
a.
Mary...friendly...Jane   Mary looks friendly and Jane does too.
He...student...she   He looks like a student and she does too.

1. Mary...beautiful...Sue   4. algebra...hard...geometry
2. a ring...expensive...a watch   5. Bob...healthy...Ralph
3. Joe...engineer...Jim

b.   LOOK and LOOK LIKE with BUT.

Examples: Teacher   Student

the teacher...young...the dentist   The teacher looks young, but the
                                         dentist doesn't.

Jim...young man...Tom   Jim looks like a young man, but
                                         Tom doesn't.

it...rain yesterday...today   It looked like rain yesterday, but
                                         it doesn't today.

1. an elephant...big...a mouse   4. Jane...movie star...Sue
2. Mary...frightened...Tom   5. it...cloudy yesterday...today
3. it...rain today...yesterday

Exercise 20.12   BEFORE, DURING, AFTER.

Examples: <u>Teacher</u>   <u>Student</u>

go to the post office...write a   I should go to the post office after I
   letter   write a letter.
talk with Jane...dinner   I should talk with Jane during dinner.
study hard...take the exam   I should study hard before I take the
                                                 exam.

1. try on the coat...buy it
2. listen carefully...class
3. study Lesson 21...finish Lesson 20
4. take a shower...go to bed
5. call up Mary...pick her up
6. take a trip...vacation
7. get a certificate...finish school
8. get a reservation...go to the play

Exercise 20.13   GET IN/OUT OF, GET ON/OFF.

Examples: <u>Teacher</u>   <u>Student</u>

The girls entered the car.   There are the girls who got in the car.
The student left the bus.   There is the student who got off the bus.
The boy mounted the bicycle.   There is the boy who got on the bicycle.

1. The boys entered the car.   5. The diplomat entered the plane.
2. The man left the train.   6. The lady left the taxi.
3. The tourists left the ship.   7. The workers entered the streetcar.
4. The girl mounted the horse.   8. The professor entered the limousine.

Exercise 20.14   HOLD, KEEP.

Examples: <u>Teacher</u>   <u>Student</u>

    car...garage   He keeps his car in a garage.
    chair...lady   He holds the chair for the lady.

1. clothes...closet   4. car...driveway
2. coat...girl friend   5. books...bookcase
3. money...bank

Exercise 20.15   JUST meaning *recently;* GET THROUGH.

Examples: <u>Teacher</u>   <u>Student</u>

doing my assignment   A. I just finished doing my assignment.
                             B. I just got through doing my assignment.
eating my dinner   C. I just finished eating my dinner.
                             D. I just got through eating my dinner.

1. studying my lesson   4. making a long-distance call
2. taking a walk   5. eating lunch
3. doing the laundry

Exercise 20.16   JUST meaning *only*.

Examples: <u>Teacher</u>   <u>Student</u>

He attends six classes a day.   I just attend five classes a day.
He speaks two languages.   I just speak one language.
He can drive a truck and a car.   I can just drive a car.

1. He is taking a fifteen-week course in English.
2. He has three hobbies.
3. He is a member of two clubs.
4. He has two degrees.
5. He is correcting all of his mistakes.

Exercise 20.17   BORED WITH, MARRIED TO, SURPRISED AT, etc.

Examples: <u>Teacher</u>   <u>Student</u>

bored...play   He was bored with the play.
married...engineer   She was married to the engineer.
filled...guests   The room was filled with guests.
surprised...weather   He was surprised at the weather.
covered...papers   The floor was covered with papers.

1. bored...program   8. tired...shopping
2. surprised...war   9. pleased...appointment
3. covered...paint   10. frightened...dogs
4. accustomed...winter   11. disappointed...audience
5. acquainted...musician   12. married...architect
6. used...working   13. full...gasoline
7. afraid...dark   14. filled...water

Lesson XXI

A. Verbs with UP.
B. HAVE.
C. BRING UP, HOLD UP, GROW UP.
D. ALMOST.
E. WISH.
F. Holidays.

≡ A.1   Observe verbs with UP.[1]

Situation: Mr. and Mrs. Smith are talking about their
daughter Nancy. Nancy is lazy; she doesn't
like to clean up her room. It's late afternoon.

> Mrs. Smith: Nancy's room was very dirty this morning.
> Mr. Smith: Did you make her CLEAN her room UP?
> Mrs. Smith: Yes, I made her clean it up when she got
> home from school.

NOTE: UP means *completion*.

Exercise 21.1   Practice UP meaning *completion*.

Examples: Teacher   Student

Is Nancy's room clean now?   Yes. Mrs. Smith made her
                                 clean it up.

Did John fill the gas tank?   Yes. She made him fill it up.

1. Did John finish his homework   5. Did he finish his dinner?
   before dinner?   6. Did he wind his watch after
2. Did he eat his vegetables?   dinner?
3. Did he fill his glass with milk?   7. Did he use all the paper?
4. Did he drink all of his milk?   8. Did he fill his pen?

≡ A.2   Observe verbs with another type of UP.

Situation: It's early in the morning. John is still in bed.

> Mrs. Smith: John, it's time to GET UP. It's Independence
> Day and you have to PUT UP our flag.
> John: But, Mother, I'm so tired I can hardly STAND UP.
> Can't Nancy HANG UP the flag?
> Mrs. Smith: No, she can't. She's preparing our picnic
> lunch.

NOTE: UP means *elevate*.

NOTE TO TEACHER: [1]These verbs with UP can be used in three
patterns: Nancy CLEANED UP her room, Nancy CLEANED her room UP,
Nancy CLEANED it UP.

Exercise 21.2   Practice verbs with UP meaning *elevate*.

Examples: <u>Teacher</u>   <u>Student</u>

John put his hand in the air.   John put his hand up.
John got out of bed early this   He got up early this morning.
  morning.
John rose when the woman came   He stood up when the woman
  in.   came in.

1. John hung the telephone on the hook.
2. John put the flag on the side of the house.
3. John got out of bed at seven o'clock.
4. When John dropped his pencil, he reached down and got it.
5. John hung his coat on the coat rack.
6. Men usually rise when a lady enters the room.

≡ B.   Observe HAVE.

   Situation: Harold and Koji are on a train. They're in the
                 dining car.

   Harold: I have to go back and get my coat, Koji. Please
             HAVE the waiter bring me a ham sandwich.

   (A little later.)

   Koji: Harold, there weren't any ham sandwiches, so I had
           him bring you a hamburger.

   NOTE: HAVE means *to cause*.

Exercise 21.3 Practice HAVE.

He had the waiter bring a hamburger.
        . . . secretary read the letter
            . . . type a letter
            . . . go to the post office
            . . . call the police
            . . . mail a package
            . . . make a plane reservation
            . . . take an exam
                . . . a picture
                . . . a trip
                . . . a vacation
                . . . taxi
                . . . streetcar
                . . . bus

≡ C.   Observe GROW UP, BRING UP, and HOLD UP.

Situation: Nancy and Margaret are in a car. Nancy is driving.

Nancy: Where were you BROUGHT UP?
Margaret: I beg your pardon?
Nancy: Where were you raised? Where did you GROW UP?
Margaret: Oh! I was brought up in Arizona. I lived there until I was
            twenty-one.
(The car in front of them has stopped.)
Nancy: I wonder what's HOLDING UP traffic. The cars ahead of us
            haven't moved for ten minutes.
Margaret: When you're in a hurry, something always delays you.

Exercise 21.4   Practice GROW UP, BRING UP, HOLD UP.

a. Examples: Teacher   Student

Margaret was raised in Arizona.   She grew up in Arizona.
John was raised in a large city.   He grew up in a large city.

    1. Margaret was raised in Phoenix.
    2. Jim was raised on a small farm.
    3. Bobby was raised in a small town.
    4. Bobby was raised beside a river.

b. Examples: Teacher   Student

Margaret's aunt brought her up.   She was brought up by her aunt.
Margaret's cousin brought her up.   She was brought up by her cousin.

1. Her grandparents brought her up. 3. Her sister-in-law brought her up.
2. Her uncle brought her up.   4. Her grandfather brought her up.

c. They wondered what was holding up traffic.
          . . . what was holding them up
          . . . why the policeman held up traffic
          . . . who was holding up traffic
          . . . where the traffic was being held up
          . . . why the traffic was being held up

≡ D. Observe ALMOST.

Situation: Harold and Koji are not far from their destination.

Harold: Were you sleeping?
Koji: I was ALMOST asleep when you spoke to me.
Harold: I'm sorry. I nearly forgot to ask you to lend me some money.
Koji: Have you used up all of yours?
Harold: Almost. I only have a few pennies left.

Exercise 21.5   Practice ALMOST.

Examples: <u>Teacher</u>   <u>Student</u>

June will be ready in five minutes.   She's almost ready.
Paul has ninety-five cents.   He has almost a dollar.

1. Jimmy will be five years old next week.
2. It's 7:55.
3. June's father is thirty-nine years old.
4. The new theater will hold 7,900 people.
5. Nine of the ten students in our class are here.
6. The train will soon be here.
7. John got 99 on his final examination.
8. The ticket cost $4.98.
9. James was very, very sick.
10. James is much better.

≡ E.   Observe WISH.

> Koji: Harold, do you know what I WISH? I wish our vaca-
>   tion started today.
> Harold: I wish we never had to go back to school.
> Koji: Why wish for the impossible?
> Harold: I'm only joking. What I really wish is that we
>   could go to school seven days a week.

NOTE: WISH expresses a desire that is contrary to fact.

Exercise 21.6   Practice WISH.

Examples: <u>Teacher</u>   <u>Student</u>

I don't have much money.   I wish I had a lot of money.
I don't know where to find my book.   I wish I knew where to find my book.
I don't know which suit to wear.   I wish I knew which suit to wear.
I don't know how to speak good   I wish I knew how to speak good
English.   English.

1. I don't know where to find my book.
2. I don't know how to speak five languages.
3. I don't know how to drive a car.
4. I don't know what to do.
5. I don't know where to eat.
6. I don't know what to say to my hostess.
7. I don't know which suit to buy.
8. I don't know which college to attend.
9. I don't know where to spend my vacation.
10. I don't know what to do this evening.

≡ F.   Holidays.

Situation: Harold and Koji are talking about holidays in the United States.

Koji: What holidays do you observe in the United States?
Harold: We have two kinds, major holidays and minor holidays.

Koji: Tell me about the major holidays.
Harold: Well, the first one is January first or New Year's Day and
the second one, Easter Sunday, commemorates the
resurrection of Christ. It's usually in April.

Koji: What's the next one?
Harold: Memorial Day or, as it is sometimes called, Decoration Day.
It is always on May thirtieth.

Koji: Why do you celebrate Memorial Day?
Harold: We celebrate it in memory of all the American men and
women who have died in war.

Koji: It must be a solemn day.
Harold: It is for many people. For example, in Washington they have
a special service at the tomb of the Unknown Soldier. In
addition, many people put flowers on the graves of their
relatives and friends.

Koji: What's the next big holiday?
Harold: The Fourth of July or Independence Day. It's the anniversary
of the Declaration of Independence.

Koji: I know. We studied about that. It was signed in 1776, wasn't it?
Harold: Right. Almost everybody puts up a flag on this day, there
are parades and in the evening there's usually an impres-
sive display of fireworks.

Koji: What's the next holiday after Independence Day?
Harold: Labor Day, the first Monday in September.

Koji: Do you celebrate it in any particular way?
Harold: No, but since it's the last holiday of summer, people like to
spend it in the country, in the mountains, or at the beach.

Koji: Thanksgiving comes next, doesn't it?
Harold: Yes. It's on the fourth Thursday of November. It was first
celebrated by the Pilgrims in 1621 to give thanks to God
for His protection and blessings. People often go to
church in the morning and have a big turkey dinner in the
afternoon. They usually invite their friends and relatives
to have dinner with them, and some families like to invite
strangers to their homes.

Koji: The last major holiday is Christmas, isn't it?
Harold: Yes, it is. Christmas is the day when we commemorate the
birth of Christ.

Koji: How is it celebrated?
Harold: Many homes put up Christmas trees and trim them with
brightly colored lights. Gifts are exchanged and many
kinds of food are prepared. The night before Christmas,
Christmas Eve, is especially important to children, because that is when Santa Claus brings them presents.

Review questions.

1. Did Mrs. Smith make Nancy clean up her room?
2. Did John want to get up early on Independence Day?
3. Do you think Mrs. Smith persuaded John to get up?
4. Did Mrs. Smith ask Nancy to put up the flag?
5. Did Koji have the waiter bring a ham sandwich for Harold?
6. What did Nancy wonder?
7. What did Harold wish?
8. Do people usually invite their friends and relatives to dinner on Thanksgiving Day?
9. Have you seen Independence Day celebrated in America?
10. Do you know which course to take next?

Lesson XXII

A. Verbs with OVER.
B. PUT OUT, TURN ON, HAND IN, etc.
C. TAKE OUT, MAKE UP, REFER TO, etc.
D. TAKE UP, BRING UP, CALL ON, etc.
E. A Letter to a University.

≡ A.1   Observe GO OVER, LOOK OVER, THINK OVER, TALK OVER.[1]

Situation: Margaret is talking with John about a new car.

> Margaret: I want to buy a new car next week, but I don't
> know very much about cars. Will you come
> with me and LOOK them OVER?
> John: Yes, I'll be glad to. Have you thought about what
> kind of car you want?
>
> Margaret: Yes, I've THOUGHT it OVER, but I haven't
> decided yet.
> John: Then I think we ought to TALK OVER the advantages
> and disadvantages of the different cars before you
> decide. If we can, we should also GO OVER the
> legal papers.

NOTE: GO OVER means *examine generally;* LOOK OVER
means *examine visually;* THINK OVER means
examine mentally; TALK OVER means *discuss.*

Exercise 22.1   Practice LOOK OVER, THINK OVER, TALK OVER.

Example: <u>Teacher</u>   <u>Student</u>

What should you have done before   I should have looked it over.
you bought that used car?
(examine visually)

1. What should Sue have done before she rented an apartment? (discuss)
2. How could Bill have done better on the exam? (examine mentally)
3. What might Jim have done before he bought his books? (examine
   visually)
4. What should Mr. Smith have done before he voted "Yes"?(examine
   mentally)
5. How could Jim have given a better speech? (discuss)
6. What should you have done before you answered the examination
   questions? (examine visually)

NOTE TO TEACHER: [1]Observe the pattern: LOOK it OVER, THINK it
OVER, TALK it OVER; but GO OVER it.

145

≡ A.2   Observe verbs with OVER.

Situation: Nancy and John are listening to records. John is also doing his homework.

Nancy: I like that record, John. Please play it OVER.
John: If I play it over, I'll make mistakes on my homework; then I'll have to do it over.
Nancy: Please play it over, John. I want to hear it again.

Exercise 22.2   Practice OVER meaning *again*.

Examples: <u>Teacher</u>   <u>Student</u>

Mary sang the song again.   She sang it over.
The student typed the report a   He typed it over.
    second time.
Jack wrote the letter again.   He wrote it over.

1. John decided to type his report   6. The students did their homework
    again.   twice.
2. Janet said the sentence again.   7. They played the record again.
3. Paul had to do the lesson again.   8. Mary sang the song twice.
4. Mr. Jones wrote the explana-   9. Jack wrote the letter again.
    tion again.   10. Mr. Jones painted the house
5. The woman washed the shirts   again.
    again.

≡ A.3   Observe RUN OVER, GET OVER, TAKE OVER.

Situation: Mr. Jones has been hit by a car. John is visiting him at the hospital.

John: I understand you were in an accident.
Mr. Jones: Yes, a car went through a red light, knocked me down and RAN OVER my glasses.

John: Will you have to have an operation?
Mr. Jones: No, the doctor said I would GET OVER my injuries without one because I only have a few cuts and bruises, and a slight headache.

John: Will you lose any of your salary while you're in the hospital?
Mr. Jones: No, your father said he would TAKE OVER my job while I'm unable to work.

Exercise 22.3   Practice RUN OVER, GET OVER, TAKE OVER.

Examples:	Teacher	Student

The car could have broken his leg. (run over)   The car could have run over his leg.

Mr. Jones should have gotten well. (get over)   Mr. Jones should have gotten over his injuries.

1. Mr. Smith should have done Mr. Jones's job. (take **over)**
2. The car might have hurt the dog's leg. (run over)
3. Jack could have gotten better. (get over)
4. He might have driven through some broken glass. (run over)
5. The new teacher should have accepted the job. (take over)
6. The truck could have killed the dog. (run over)

≡ B.   Observe PUT OUT, TURN ON, HAND IN, etc.

Situation: John and his mother are driving home from the city.

> Mrs. Smith: Please PUT OUT your cigarette. It makes me nervous
>   to see someone drive and smoke at the same time.
> John: All right. Smoking is bad for me anyway.
>
> Mrs. Smith: Please TURN OFF the radio. It's giving me a headache.
> John: Yes, mother. The program isn't very good anyway.
>
> Mrs. Smith: Can I PUT AWAY this map?
> John: Yes. I'm through with it.
>
> Mrs. Smith: Let's CALL OFF our card party for tonight. I have to
>   FILL OUT an application for that job at the dormitory.
>
> John: When do you plan to HAND it IN?
> Mrs. Smith: Early next week. It's very long, but the office manager
>   said I could LEAVE OUT the last two pages.
>
> John: How long ago did he HAND OUT the applications?
> Mrs. Smith: About two weeks ago. John, shouldn't you TURN ON
>   your lights? It's getting dark.

Exercise 22.4   Use two-word verbs to answer the following questions.

1. What did John do with his cigarette?
2. What did John do to the radio?
3. What did Mrs. Smith do with the map?
4. Who wanted to call off the card party?
5. What should Mrs. Smith do with the job application before she hands it in?
6. What is she going to do with it after she fills it out?
7. What could Mrs. Smith do with the last two pages?
8. When it was getting dark, what did she say to John?
9. What did the office manager do with the job applications?
10. What would John do if he wanted to listen to the radio?
11. What does John do to the lights before he goes to bed?
12. Does John take off his clothes when he gets up in the morning?
13. What does John do before he buys a coat?

≡ C.   Observe TAKE OUT, MAKE UP, REFER TO, CHECK OUT.

Situation: John is at the city library.

> John: I can't decide which books to TAKE OUT.
> Librarian: Perhaps I can help you MAKE UP your mind.
>
> John: Do you have any books on the Civil War?
> Librarian: Yes, we have several. This is a good one about military battles. The authors of these books REFER TO some of the problems of the Civil War. And those books are related to the results of the Civil War.
>
> John: Thank you. I'd like to CHECK OUT one of each.

Exercise 22.5   Practice TAKE OUT, MAKE UP, REFER TO, etc.

Examples: <u>Teacher</u>   <u>Student</u>

He couldn't decide which books were   He couldn't make up his mind
   best. (make up his mind)   which books were best.
John wanted to borrow some library   John wanted to take out some
   books. (take out)   library books.

1. One author wrote a few words about a locomotive. (refer to)
2. Some books told about the results of the Civil War. (be related to)
3. John left the library with three books. (check out)
4. Several authors mentioned the problems of the Civil War. (refer to)
5. Mary decided to go to Florida. (make up her mind)
6. Mrs. Jones can't decide how many oranges to buy. (make up her mind)

≡ D.   Observe TAKE UP, BRING UP, CALL ON, PUT OFF, BLOW OUT,
        etc.

   Situation: Ali is a student at the English Language Institute. He is in
              a vocabulary class.

Teacher: Today we're going to TAKE UP the subject of birthdays.
          Please BRING UP your questions whenever you think of
          them so that I can CALL ON you. I will answer most of
          them today, but I may have to PUT OFF some until
          tomorrow.

Ali: I'd like to ask a question. What is a birthday cake?

Teacher: It's a cake that the child's mother bakes for the birthday
          celebration. She usually decorates the cake and puts
          one candle on it for each year of the child's age.

          For the celebration, everybody sings Happy Birthday to the
          child, someone lights the candles with a match and the
          lights are turned off. Then the child makes a wish, and
          before the candles BURN UP, she tries to BLOW them
          all OUT. If she blows them out with one breath, her
          wish is supposed to come true.

          I wish we had more time so that I could answer more
          questions. Tomorrow I'll POINT OUT a few more
          things about birthdays.

   Exercise 22.6   Practice TAKE UP, BRING UP, CALL ON, etc.

      Examples: <u>Teacher</u>   <u>Student</u>

      The teacher often questions the   The teacher often calls on the
        students. (call on)   students.
      The students can also ask ques-   The students can also bring
        tions. (bring up)   up questions.

   1. The teacher might discuss their questions. (take up)
   2. The teacher might postpone their questions until later. (put off)
   3. The teacher might ask someone to give an answer. (call on)
   4. A student might give an important fact. (point out)
   5. The fire destroyed everything. (burn up)
   6. The wind extinguished every match he lit. (blow out)
   7. Students often postpone work until the last moment. (put off)

≡ E.   A Letter to Central University.

1022 Hill Street
Ann Arbor, Michigan
May 15, 1965

School of Business Administration
Central University
Central, Nebraska

Gentlemen:

I am interested in applying for admission to Central University, School of Business Administration. At the present time, I am accepted for the Fall semester at Riverside University. I plan to study there for two years and then I would like to transfer to Central University. I would like to know the requirements for admission so that I can plan my program at Riverside University. Any information that you can give me will be appreciated.

Sincerely yours,

Ali Yazback

Review questions.

1. Why should John have looked over the cars for Margaret?
2. Why might John have played the record over?
3. Should the car have gone through the red light?
4. Where must the injured man have been taken?
5. What could John have been asking the librarian?
6. What did the teacher wish she could have done?
7. Why might John have put out his cigarette?
8. Who should have done his homework last night?

Lesson XXIII

A. Verbs with ON.
B. WHENEVER, IF, UNLESS, ALTHOUGH, BECAUSE.
C. Verbs with BACK.
D. Deceptive Cognates.
E. Freshman and Sophomore Courses.

≡ A.1   Observe verbs with ON.

Situation: The Smith family is taking a trip to Phoenix, Arizona.

> Mr. Smith: Should we stop in Reno, or GO ON to Las Vegas?
>
> Mrs. Smith: We had better stop. Our gas tank is almost empty and
> we don't want to run out of gas in the middle of the
> desert.
>
> Mr. Smith: We'll definitely gas up in Reno, but should we stay
> there or DRIVE ON? How many want to continue?
>
> John: I do. Since we're in a hurry to get to Phoenix, I think we
> should TRAVEL ON to Las Vegas.

NOTE: ON means *continue*.

Exercise 23.1   Practice ON meaning *continue*.

a. Examples: <u>Teacher</u>   <u>Student</u>

Pete slept until noon. (go on)   Pete slept until noon before he
                                                         went on.

He stopped at Reno, Nevada.   He stopped at Reno, Nevada
   (drive on)   before he drove on.

He stayed in Denver, Colorado.   He stayed in Denver, Colorado
   (go on)   before he went on.

   1. He rested in Chicago. (fly on)
   2. He stopped at Lake Michigan. (travel on)
   3. He sat down on the grass. (walk on)
   4. He rested for two days on an island. (sail on)
   5. He stayed one night in New York. (fly on)

b. Examples: <u>Teacher</u>   <u>Student</u>

He won't get to Reno. (drive on)   He won't get to Reno unless
                                                         he drives on.

He won't reach Tokyo. (fly on)   He won't reach Tokyo unless
                                                         he flies on.

   1. We won't reach San Francisco. (sail on)
   2. We won't get there by eight. (drive on)
   3. They won't reach home in time for dinner. (walk on)
   4. They won't get enough rest. (sleep on)
   5. They won't get the car repaired. (work on)

151

≡ A.2   Observe WAIT ON, TRY ON, DEPEND ON, etc.

Situation: John is buying a new coat.

Salesman: May I WAIT ON you?
John: Yes. I'd like to TRY ON some sport coats. I prefer something
      like the one I HAVE ON.
Salesman: PUT this one ON. It's a popular style and the material is
      excellent. You can DEPEND ON it to last a long time.

John: Fine. I'm going to CALL ON my girl friend this afternoon, and
      she INSISTS ON good clothes.
Salesman: Shall I put it in a box, or do you want to KEEP it ON?
John: I think I'll wear it. You can put my old coat in a box.

NOTE: KEEP ON means *continue to wear*.

Exercise 23.2   Practice WAIT ON, HAVE ON, DEPEND ON.

Examples: Teacher	Student
John is wearing a raincoat because of the rain. (have on)	John has a raincoat on because of the rain.
John will visit his girl friend regardless of the weather. (call on)	John will call on his girl friend regardless of the weather.

1. The salesman must serve John in spite of his headache. (wait on)
2. John intends to wear his new coat in place of his old one. (keep on)
3. John will put on the coat regardless of its cost. (try on)
4. He wants this coat because of its style. (insists on)
5. John can be sure of the quality. (depend on)
6. John might visit his girl friend in spite of her father. (call on)
7. John is wearing gloves because of the cold weather. (have on)

≡ B.1   Observe WHENEVER.

Situation: Mr. Smith and Mr. Jones are talking about vacations.

Mr. Smith: What do you like to do WHENEVER you have a vacation?
Mr. Jones: I like to go on trips. I am always ready to travel.

Mr. Smith: I wish I could say that. Whenever I have a vacation I
      have to either repair my car or visit relatives.

NOTE: WHENEVER means *any time, every time*.

Exercise 23.3   Practice WHENEVER.

Examples: Teacher	Student
be ready to go—cab gets here	I'll be ready to go whenever the cab gets here.
like to study—have time	I like to study whenever I have time.

1. like to take a trip—have a vacation
2. like to go for a drive—can
3. don't like noise—have a headache
4. have to work on my car—can find enough time
5. want you to study—you can
6. have to run to class—get up late
7. usually put on my coat—the weather is cold

≡ B.2   Observe IF and UNLESS.

Situation: Nancy is talking with her brother John.

Nancy: Is your friend Jim going to college?
John: Yes, IF he can afford it.

Nancy: Is he going to attend the state university or a private university?
John: He intends to go to a private university UNLESS it's too expensive.

NOTES: IF means *provided that, in case that.*
UNLESS means *if . . . not.*

Exercise 23.4   Practice IF and UNLESS.

Examples: Teacher   Student

Are you going to college?—can afford it
                    —too expensive

A. Yes, I am if I can afford it.
B. Yes, I am unless it's too expensive.

Are you going to the concert?—clear
                    —rains

C. Yes, I am if it's clear.
D. Yes, I am unless it rains.

1. Are you going to see your adviser?—in his office
                    —out of his office
2. Are you going to see the doctor?—can see me
                    —too busy
3. Can you finish your assignment?—easy enough
                    —too hard
4. Are you going to buy a new car?—cheap enough
                    —too expensive
5. Do you like to swim?—warm enough
                    —too cold

≡ B.3   Observe ALTHOUGH and BECAUSE.

Situation: Billy Smith and his friend Bobby are fishing.

Billy: Why do you want to go to college when you grow up?
Bobby: BECAUSE I want to be a scientist.

Billy: My brother told me that you have to study very hard when
        you're in college.
Bobby: Maybe. But you know, ALTHOUGH everyone says that,
        many students must not believe it because they never
        seem to study. At least, my brother doesn't.

NOTES: BECAUSE means *for the reason that, due to the fact that.*
       ALTHOUGH means *even if, in spite of the fact that.*

Exercise 23.5   Practice ALTHOUGH and BECAUSE.

Examples: Teacher   Student

He studied hard—had an exam   He studied hard because he had an
                                       exam.
He went to bed early—wasn't   He went to bed early although he
sleepy   wasn't sleepy.

1. He wanted a new car—didn't have much money
2. He bought some new clothes—needed them
3. He made good grades—studied very hard
4. He called up his friend—wanted to borrow some money
5. He looked up his friend's phone number—had forgotten it
6. He sat down—preferred to stand
7. He never gets up early—likes to sleep
8. He spoke only English—preferred to speak Spanish
9. He closed the door—wanted to be alone
10. He went to the concert—would rather see a play

≡ C.   Observe verbs with BACK.

Situation: John is talking to Pedro.

John: How long are you going to stay in the United States?
Pedro: For two more months. I have to GO BACK to Mexico in
        November.

John: Are you going to FLY BACK or DRIVE BACK?
Pedro: It would be too expensive to fly back, so I'll have to
        drive back.

NOTE: BACK with verbs like go, fly, drive, walk means *return.*

Exercise 23.6   Practice BACK meaning *return*.

a. Examples: <u>Teacher</u>   <u>Student</u>

He ran to the bus station.   He ran to the bus station, but he
                                    walked back.

He walked to the theater.   He walked to the theater, but he
                                    rode back.

1. He drove to New York.   4. He sailed to Hawaii.
2. He flew to San Francisco.   5. He rode to the mountains.
3. He ran to the store.

b. Example: <u>Teacher</u>   <u>Student</u>

   drove the car—to Mexico   He drove the car back to
                                    Mexico.

1. got the pencil—from his friend   4. sent the dog—to its owner
2. gave the book—to Mary   5. took the car—to the
3. flew the plane—to Venezuela   garage

≡ D. Observe REGISTER, FACULTY, UNIVERSITY, etc.

Situation: John and Jim are having a soda together.

John: When do you REGISTER at the state UNIVERSITY?
Jim: On September fourth.

John: I understand that the teachers in the engineering department
          are excellent.
Jim: Yes, their FACULTY includes many famous professors.

John: What other reasons made you choose the state university?
Jim: Just one. TUITION is much cheaper at a PUBLIC COLLEGE
          than at a PRIVATE college.

NOTES: REGISTER means *become a student*.
       FACULTY means *the teachers*.
       COLLEGE means *an institution of higher learning,
          beyond high school*.
       UNIVERSITY usually includes several separate departments,
          schools, or colleges.
       PRIVATE means *not operated by the state*.
       PUBLIC means *operated by the state*.
       TUITION means *the money paid by students for their
          instruction*.

≡ E. Freshman and Sophomore Courses.

> Ali: Hello, Professor Jones. I'd like to talk with you about my pro-
> gram of studies for this semester.
> Professor: Come in, Ali. You're enrolling as a freshman, aren't
> you? Usually your freshman and sophomore years
> are devoted to general studies in six different areas.
> You will need to take between fifteen and twenty
> courses during these two years.
>
> Ali: What are the six areas, sir?
> Professor: English composition, foreign languages, mathematics and
> philosophy, humanities, social sciences, and natural
> sciences.
>
> Ali: What do you advise me to take?
> Professor: First of all, you should take English composition. Since
> English is not your native language, it will also satisfy
> your foreign language requirement.
>
> Ali: Do I have a choice between math and philosophy?
> Professor: Yes. Since you are going to major in business adminis-
> tration, you should choose math.
>
> Ali: What shall I take in the humanities?
> Professor: You have a choice of literature, fine arts, and music. Why
> don't you take the introductory course in English
> literature?
>
> Ali: All right. In the social sciences, I'd like to take economics. I
> think it will be more useful to me than anthropology or political
> science. What course do you recommend in the natural sciences?
>
> Professor: Well, instead of zoology, botany, physics, or astronomy, I
> think psychology would be the most useful for you.
>
> Ali: Let me see. So far I have five courses: English composition,
> English literature, math, economics and psychology. What
> else should I take?
> Professor: That's enough. Each course is three hours, and fifteen
> hours is a full schedule.
>
> Ali: When do I pay my tuition?
> Professor: When you register.
> Ali: Thank you.
> Professor: Good luck. Feel free to call on me at any time during
> the semester.

Review questions.

1. Why did John think they should go on to Las Vegas?
2. Why did John like the new sport coat?
3. When does Mr. Smith repair his car or visit relatives?
4. Will Jim go to college?
5. Will Jim attend a private university?
6. Why does Bobby want to go to college?
7. Did Bobby think that college students study hard?
8. Which course will Ali take in place of political science?

Lesson XXIV

A. Verbs with ABOUT.
B. The University.

☰ A.   Observe verbs with ABOUT.

Situation: John is talking with his father about attending a university.

> Mr. Smith: Have you decided whether or not you want to go to college
> next fall?
> John: Yes, I have, Dad. I've THOUGHT ABOUT it a lot and I
> definitely want to.
>
> Mr. Smith: Have you decided which university you want to go to?
> John: No, not yet. I intend to TALK with my adviser ABOUT the
> different universities tomorrow. I also plan to WRITE to
> some of them ABOUT scholarships.

NOTE: ABOUT means *regarding*.

Exercise 24.1   Practice verbs with ABOUT meaning *regarding*.

a. Example: Teacher   Student

We would have been happy with   We would have been happy
your decision. (know about)   with your decision if we
                                       had known about it.

1. Mary might have understood the assignment. (ask about)
2. He would have remembered the answer. (think about)
3. They might have understood the problems. (talk about)
4. I could have given a better speech. (think about)

b. Examples: Teacher   Student

talk—a boy who went to college   He talked about a boy who went to
                                   college.

worry—a classmate who was sick   He worried about a classmate who
                                   was sick.

1. dream—a man who spoke only English
2. wrote—a boy who looked for a frog
3. talk--a family who went to Arizona
4. think--the students who were learning English
5. worry—the student who went to the hospital
6. wonder—the relatives who were coming
7. sing—two young people who were in love

≡ B.1   Observe CATALOGUE, TIME SCHEDULE.

Situation: Ali is talking with John Smith.

Ali: I'm supposed to register at the University next week, but I don't
       know where to find a description of the courses or the cost of
       tuition.
John: Why don't you get a CATALOGUE?

Ali: Does each school in the university have a catalogue?
John: Usually. If you're interested in engineering, you should obtain
       one from the school of engineering.

Ali: Does the catalogue also give the time, place, and name of the
       instructor for each course?
John: No. The TIME SCHEDULE contains that information.

Exercise 24.2   Answer the questions.

   1. What gives a description of each course?
   2. What gives the time and place of each course?
   3. How do you find out what the courses are like?
   4. How do you find out the hour and room number of each course?

≡ B.2   Observe RECITATION CLASS, LAB CLASS, LECTURE CLASS,
          SEMINAR.

Situation: Ali has picked up his time schedule and is talking
             with his adviser.

Ali: Would you please explain these abbreviations in the
       time schedule to me?
Prof. Jones: Of course. REC means RECITATION CLASS.
               The teacher talks informally and calls on
               students to answer questions. The students
               can also raise questions and bring up problems.

Ali: What does LAB mean?
Prof. Jones: It means LABORATORY CLASS. The student
               may work with machines, or he may do
               experiments and write reports about them.

Ali: What about LEC?
Prof. Jones: That stands for LECTURE CLASS. A profes-
               sor gives lectures and the students take notes.

Ali: The last abbreviation is SEM.
Prof. Jones: It stands for SEMINAR. The professor and the
               class, usually graduate students, discuss
               problems related to a specific subject. The
               students frequently prepare reports and
               sometimes read them to the rest of the class.

Exercise 24.3   Answer the questions.

1. What kind of class is this?
2. What other kinds of classes do you have?
3. In what kind of class does the professor speak and the students take notes?
4. In what kind of class do the students and the professor sit around a table and discuss the special problems of a subject?
5. What do students do in a laboratory class?
6. What does a professor do in a lecture class?
7. What do students frequently do in a seminar class?
8. What does an instructor do in a recitation class?
9. What can the students do in a recitation class?

☰ B.3   Observe JUNIOR, SENIOR; Degrees.

Situation: Ali is walking home from school with Nancy Smith.

Ali: This year as a freshman and next year as a sophomore I have to take courses in five general areas.
Nancy: That's right. Then in your third and fourth years, as a JUNIOR and a SENIOR, you will be able to concentrate on your major.
Ali: When can I expect to get a BACHELOR'S DEGREE?
Nancy: In about four years or after you have taken 120 hours. Do you plan to go on for a MASTER'S DEGREE after your bachelor's?
Ali: Yes, and I also hope to get a DOCTOR'S DEGREE. I suppose that will be about ten years from now.

Exercise 24.4   Answer the questions.

1. Frank has his high school diploma. He's going to begin his first year at the university. What is he?
2. Frank has finished his freshman year. He's beginning his second year. What is he?
3. Frank has finished his sophomore year. He's beginning his third year. What is he?
4. Frank has finished his junior year. He's beginning his fourth year. What is he?
5. Frank has just finished his senior year. What degree does he have?
6. Frank is studying for a master's degree. What kind of student is he?
7. Frank has finished his first year of graduate school. He expects to receive a degree. What degree is it?
8. Frank has studied several years as a graduate student. This June he expects to receive a degree. What degree is it?

≡ B.4   Observe TEXTBOOK, REFERENCE BOOK.

Situation: Ali meets Jim near the bookstore.

Ali: Is it necessary to buy many books for each course?

Jim: No, you only need to buy the TEXTBOOK. The teacher assigns
      homework in it regularly during the term.

Ali: Does a teacher make assignments in any other books?

Jim: Yes, he also makes special assignments in REFERENCE BOOKS,
      but you don't have to buy them. They are available in the
      library and you can check them out for a few hours or over-
      night whenever you like.

Exercise 24.5   Answer the questions.

1. What kind of book is used regularly during a course?
2. What kind of book do you check out of the library?
3. Which book should students buy?
4. What are textbooks used for?
5. What are the reference books used for?
6. Do students have to buy reference books?
7. Can they buy them if they want to?

≡ B.5   Observe COMPOSITION, TERM PAPER, THESIS DISSERTATION.

Situation: Ali is visiting Mr. Smith.

Ali: Mr. Smith, what kind of written assignments may be made
      during a course?

Mr. Smith: Several different kinds. For example, in elementary
            courses you usually have to write short COMPOSITIONS
            about specific subjects. Sometimes one composition
            is assigned every week.

Ali: And in advanced courses?

Mr. Smith: In advanced courses you usually have to write one or two
            TERM PAPERS. Each of them should be ten or more
            pages long.

Ali: Is a term paper the same as a THESIS?

Mr. Smith: No, a thesis requires much more research and is usually
            a lot longer. It is often a requirement for a master's
            degree.

Ali: I suppose a DISSERTATION requires even more research than
      a thesis.

Mr. Smith: Yes, it does. It is one of the requirements for a doctor's
            degree.

Exercise 24.6   Answer the questions.

1. What kind of written assignment is required in an elementary course?
2. What kind is required in an advanced course?
3. How many written assignments do professors usually make each semester?
4. What kinds of papers do graduate students have to write?
5. What is usually one requirement for a master's degree?
6. What is the difference between a dissertation and a composition?
7. What is the difference between a thesis and a term paper?

☰ B.6   Observe FINAL, MIDTERM, TEST, QUIZ.

Situation: Ali is talking with Mrs. Smith.

Ali: Do all university courses have examinations?
Mrs. Smith: No, but almost all of them do and there are usually two of them. The one given in the middle of a course is called a MIDTERM exam. The other one is given at the end of the course and is called the FINAL exam.

Ali: Are there any others besides these?
Mrs. Smith: Well, some teachers also give short exams, but these are called TESTS or QUIZZES.

Ali: What does a student's final grade depend on?
Mrs. Smith: It depends on everything: on the examinations, quizzes, written assignments, and often on attendance.

Exercise 24.7   Please answer the questions.

1. What kinds of examinations are given during a university course?
2. When are midterms given?
3. When is the final given?
4. What is the difference between a test and an exam?
5. What does a student's final grade depend on?

Review questions.

1. What might John get if he writes to several universities?
2. Should Ali get a Time Schedule before or after he registers?
3. What type of class should Ali attend if he wants to take notes?
4. What does Ali expect to get after he has taken 120 hours?
5. Would Ali have bought a textbook or a reference book if he had taken a course in mathematics?
6. What will Ali's final grade depend on if he takes a course in English composition?

Lesson XXV

A. Communications.

___

≡ A.1   Observe PUBLICATION, LOCAL, DEVOTE, SPACE.

Situation: John and his friend Pedro, who is visiting the United States, pass a newsstand on the way home from a walk around town.

John: Let's stop at this newsstand, Pedro. I promised my father that I'd bring him a copy of the Sunday Times.

Pedro: You mean the New York Times, don't you? I've seen it on sale in every city I've visited.

John: Yes. It's a very popular newspaper.

Pedro: Isn't it an official government PUBLICATION?

John: No, we don't have any official newspaper in the United States; that is, we don't have any one newspaper that expresses the opinion of the entire country.

Pedro: Do you mean that you have only privately owned newspapers?

John: Yes, that's right. And they are all LOCAL, except for papers like the Christian Science Monitor. Some of them, however, like the New York Times and the Chicago Tribune, DEVOTE most of their SPACE to national news and only a small part of it to local New York or Chicago news.

NOTES: DEVOTE means *set aside*.
         SPACE indicates *columns or pages in the newspaper*.

Exercise 25.1   Answer the questions.

1. Where were John and Pedro returning from?
2. Where did they stop?
3. Why did they stop there?
4. What did John want to buy?
5. Which newspaper had Pedro seen on sale everywhere in the United States?
6. Is the New York Times an official government publication?
7. What kind of newspapers are found in the United States?
8. What kind of news is found in the New York Times?
9. Does it devote any space to news about New York?
10. Can the New York Times be thought of as a national newspaper?

☰ A.2　　Observe SUBSCRIBE TO, DO WITHOUT.

Pedro: Does your family SUBSCRIBE TO any newspapers?
John: Yes, we take a local paper. We could also subscribe to the
　　　New York Times for the Sunday edition, but we don't.

Pedro: Then you have to pick it up every Sunday, don't you?
John: Yes; but I don't mind.

Pedro: Could you ever DO WITHOUT the Sunday paper?
John: I think I could, but my father couldn't. He always has to have
　　　his Sunday Times.

　　Exercise 25.2　　Answer the questions.

　　　1. What does John's family subscribe to?
　　　2. Do they subscribe to the New York Times?
　　　3. Could they take only the Sunday edition of the Times if they
　　　　　wanted to?
　　　4. How do they get their Sunday paper?
　　　5. Could John do without the Sunday paper?
　　　6. Could his father?

☰ A.3　　Observe ASK FOR, RUN.

Pedro: I wonder if they have the Detroit Free Press?
John: I don't know. Why don't you ASK FOR it?

Pedro: I think I will. Do you see the newsboy anywhere?
John: That's him over there. He's waiting on that lady in the blue
　　　dress.

Pedro: I'll wait until he finishes with her. She seems to be buying
　　　several newspapers and magazines.

John: She always does. She RUNS that beauty parlor across the
　　　street.
Pedro: Does she own it?

John: No, she just manages it.
Pedro: Well, here he comes at last. Let's get him to wait on us be-
　　　fore anyone else comes.

John: Do you remember what you were going to ask for?
Pedro: Of course! The . . . No, come to think of it, I guess I don't.

NOTES: ASK FOR means *request.*
　　　　RUN means *manage.*

Exercise 25.3   Answer the questions.

1. What did Pedro wonder?
2. What did he think he'd do?
3. What was the newsboy doing?
4. Why was the lady in the blue dress buying so many papers and magazines?
5. Did she own the beauty shop?
6. What happened when the newsboy came to wait on Pedro and John?

≡ A.4   Observe PUBLISH, CONTAIN, ISSUE, INCLUDE.

John: Let's look at the magazines while we're here.

Pedro: All right. There certainly are a lot of them PUBLISHED in the United States. How can Americans ever find time to read them all?

John: They don't, Pedro. Most people read only two or three of them regularly. We, for example, take a news magazine and a general interest magazine. Father, of course, subscribes to a special interest one.

Pedro: By news magazine you're referring to Time, Newsweek, the Nation, and the New Republic, aren't you?

John: Yes, and I was also thinking of Current. It CONTAINS several different points of view about the basic problems and ISSUES of a democratic society.

Pedro: And by general interest magazine I suppose you mean the Reader's Digest and the Saturday Evening Post.

John: Yes, I do; but I would also INCLUDE Harper's and the New Yorker.

Pedro: What do you mean by a special interest magazine?

John: One of these. You see, each of these magazines is devoted to a hobby and a specific activity; for example, fishing, movies, and business. There must be a magazine here for every interest you can think of.

Exercise 25.4   Answer the following questions.

1. Are many magazines published in the United States?
2. What kind of magazines are they?
3. How many do most people read regularly?
4. How many news magazines can you think of?
5. What kinds of issues are they devoted to?
6. How many general interest magazines can you think of?
7. What kind of articles do they contain?
8. Do they include news articles?
9. What is a special interest magazine?
10. How many special interest magazines can you think of?

≡ A.5   Observe MEANS OF COMMUNICATION, NETWORK,
         INFORMATIVE.

Situation: Pedro and John leave the newsstand and continue on their
             way home.

Pedro: It seems to me that most people in the United States depend
         on the papers and the magazines for international news.

John: Yes, I think you can say that. However, there is one other
        MEANS OF COMMUNICATION that is becoming very im-
        portant.

Pedro: You're thinking of television, aren't you?

John: Yes, I am. We have three major NETWORKS: The National
        Broadcasting Company (NBC), the Columbia Broadcasting
        System (CBS), and the American Broadcasting Company (ABC).

Pedro: Do you remember when radios were as popular as TV sets
         are now?

John: Yes, I remember listening to all sorts of programs on the
        radio. Now I only listen to it for music, unless I'm on a
        trip. Then I listen to whatever I can find.

Pedro: I enjoy watching the news programs on television. They are
         very INFORMATIVE in many ways.

John: Have you watched any of the Special News Reports?

Pedro: Yes. I liked one especially well, the one that showed your
         first astronaut being put into orbit around the earth.

John: I remember that one too. It was a very exciting report. Can
        you imagine what communications will be like ten years
        from now?

Pedro: No, I can't. Sometimes I wish I were a teenager once again.
         The world seems much more exciting now than it did
         when we were growing up. A few years ago a teacher
         would never have called on a student to talk about jet
         planes and satellites.

Exercise 25.5   Answer the questions.
   1. What is meant by "means of communication"?
   2. Can you name four different types?
   3. What are the three major TV networks in the United States?
   4. Is there an Educational Television network too?
   5. What sort of programs can be seen on television besides news?
   6. What sort of programs can be heard on radio?
   7. What kind of television programs do you think are the most
       informative?
   8. What kind of television programs do you think are the most
       enjoyable?
   9. What are some of the most recent developments in communi-
       cation? (Relay, Telstar, Syncom satellites.)
  10. What do you think communication will be like ten years from now?

≡ A.6   Observe CAMPUS.

John: Incidentally, would you like to go with me to a lecture on
        communications tomorrow night?

Pedro: Yes, I would. What time does it begin?
John: At eight o'clock. Shall I call for you at seven-thirty?

Pedro: No, I won't be home. Ali and I are going to call on a friend of
        ours at six-thirty. Can I meet you somewhere?

John: Yes, of course. The lecture is being given at the University.
        Do you know where the library is?

Pedro: It's at the center of the CAMPUS, isn't it?
John: Yes. I'll wait for you there. Can you make it by a quarter of
        eight?

Pedro: I'm sure I can.
John: Would Ali like to join us?
Pedro: No, he has a date.

Exercise 25.6   Answer the questions.

1. What was the lecture about?
2. Did John call for Pedro?
3. Where was the library located?
4. Why wouldn't Ali be able to join them?
5. Should Ali have taken his date to the lecture?

Review questions.

1. Did John say that the New York Times is such a popular paper that
    you can buy it anywhere in the United States?
2. Does the New York Times devote so much space to national and
    international news that it doesn't have any space left for local
    news?
3. What does Mr. Smith depend so much on that he can't do without it
    on Sundays?
4. What was Pedro so busy doing that he forgot what he wanted to ask
    for?
5. What were there such a lot of that made Pedro ask, ''How can
    Americans find time to read them all?
6. What impressed John and Pedro so much that they wished they were
    teenagers again?
7. Did the boys have such an interesting discussion that they wanted
    to continue it the next night?

Lesson XXVI

A. Verbs with WITH.
B. Geography.

≡ A. Observe verbs with WITH.

> John: Ali, tell me some of your impressions about the United
> States.
> Ali: I don't know if you'll AGREE WITH what I say, John.
>
> John: Don't worry about that. I think you see things much
> more objectively than I do.
> Ali: All right. I am very IMPRESSED WITH the number of
> things that one can enjoy and do without getting out of a
> car.
>
> John: I'd never thought about that. There are quite a few,
> aren't there? We have drive-in restaurants, drive-in
> movies, drive-in banks, and even drive-in laundries.
>
> Ali: Yes, and if you have a car, you can go to all of them.
> John: You sound as if you're SATISFIED WITH your new car.
>
> Ali: You're right, I am. They taught me everything CONNECTED
> WITH owning and driving a car when I bought it, and I
> am really enjoying it.

Exercise 26.1   Answer the following questions.

1. Did Ali think John would agree with him?
2. What was Ali impressed with?
3. What was Ali satisfied with?
4. What did they teach Ali when he bought his car?
5. Would you agree with Ali, or disagree with him?
6. What have you been impressed with about the United States?
7. Are you satisfied with everything, or disappointed with
   everything?
8. What was your funniest experience connected with learning
   English?

≡ B.1   Observe BORDER, PLAIN, DESERT, FLOW.

Ali: How was your trip to Arizona last summer, John?
John: It was excellent, Ali. When are you going to take a trip
         around the United States?

Ali: If everything works out, I'll take a trip in June.
John: Let me tell you a few things about my trip.

Ali: I wish you would.
John: First of all, our trip took several days. Did you know
         that it's about 3,000 miles from one side of the United
         States to the other and that it is about 1,200 miles
         from the Canadian BORDER to the Mexican border?

Ali: No, I didn't. Are there many mountains between New York
         and San Francisco?
John: Yes, there are. As you drive west from New York, you
         cross the Appalachian Mountains, then miles and
         miles of PLAINS, the Rocky Mountains, a DESERT and
         then more mountains.

Ali: What are the main rivers?
John: The Mississippi, the Colorado, and the Columbia. The
         Mississippi River is our most important river. It
         begins near the Canadian border and is joined by the
         Missouri River, the Ohio River and hundreds of
         others as it FLOWS toward the Gulf of Mexico.

Ali: Now tell me something about the lakes.
John: You already know about the Great Lakes: Superior,
         Michigan, Huron, Erie and Ontario. Besides those,
         there are thousands of other lakes throughout the
         United States and a large salt lake in Utah.

Exercise 26.2   Answer the following questions.

1. How far is it from the Canadian border to the Mexican border?
2. How far is it from one side of the United States to the other?
3. What are some of the mountains?
4. Are the Rocky Mountains in the East or in the West?
5. What are the three main rivers?
6. What direction does the Mississippi River flow, north or south?
7. What are the five Great Lakes?
8. Are there many other lakes in the United States?
9. What kind of lake is there in Utah?

☰ B.2   Observe ZONE, MODIFY, ANNUAL, TAKE IN.

Ali: Mr. Smith, what type of climate does the United States
         have?

Mr. Smith: That's not an easy question to answer. Although the
              United States is largely in the temperate ZONE,
              its climate is MODIFIED by both mountain ranges
              and winds.

Ali: Is the weather usually hot?

Mr. Smith: No, it isn't. The average ANNUAL temperature is
              about 75° F in the South and about 45° F in the
              North. However, the temperature sometimes
              rises to 120° in Arizona and Texas. On the other
              hand, it often drops to 40° below zero in Minne-
              sota.

Ali: I think I'll stay in this state. Tell me, when a person
         travels from New York to Los Angeles, how many times
         does he have to change his watch?

Mr. Smith: Three times. The country is divided into four time
              zones: Eastern, Central, Mountain, and Pacific
              Coast. The eastern zone TAKES IN the Atlantic
              coast and the Appalachian Mountains, the central
              zone takes in the plains area, the mountain
              zone takes in the Rocky Mountains, and the
              Pacific Coast zone covers the west coast area.

Exercise 26.3   Practice TAKE IN.

Examples: <u>Teacher</u>   <u>Student</u>

         the mountain zone . . .   The mountain zone takes in the
                                        Rocky Mountains.

         mathematics . . .   Mathematics takes in geometry,
                                        algebra, and calculus.

1. his field of study . . .   6. the study of any language . . .
2. medicine . . .   7. the study of geography . . .
3. physical science . . .   8. Europe . . .
4. natural science . . .   9. History . . .
5. Central America . . .   10. Asia . . .

≡ B.3   Observe FERTILE, EXTEND, CROP, PRINCIPAL, COMMERCIAL.

Situation: Nancy is talking with Ali about agricultural products.

Ali: What is the heart of American agriculture?

Nancy: The "corn belt," a region of very FERTILE land that
        EXTENDS from Nebraska eastward as far as
        Pennsylvania. Nebraska is also in the wheat belt; it
        extends from Texas northward to North Dakota.

Ali: Are corn and wheat the main CROPS in the South and West,
      too?

Nancy: No, cotton and tobacco are the PRINCIPAL crops in the
        South. The principal crops in the West, located
        largely in California, are fruits and COMMERCIALLY
        grown vegetables.

Exercise 26.4   Answer the following questions.

1. What and where is the corn belt?
2. What kind of land is fertile land?
3. Is the wheat belt east or west of the corn belt?
4. How far north does the wheat belt extend?
5. What are the principal products in the South?
6. What are some of the main crops in the West?

≡ B.4   Observe RESOURCE, INDUSTRY, DEPOSIT, REGION.

Situation: John is telling Ali about mineral resources.

John: Ali, did you know that one of the keys to this country's
       richness is its mineral RESOURCES?

Ali: You'll have to explain what you mean, John.

John: Well, three of the most basic needs of modern INDUSTRY
       are iron ore, coal, and petroleum, and the United
       States contains large quantities of all three. For
       example, the Appalachian Mountains, especially in
       Pennsylvania and West Virginia, contain very large
       coal DEPOSITS, the Lake Superior REGION contains
       large iron ore deposits, and the Texas-Oklahoma
       region and California contain large oil fields.

Ali: Does that mean that most of your manufacturing is located
      in those areas, too?

John: Yes, it does. If you drew a line from Boston, Massachu-
       setts to Minneapolis, Minnesota to Birmingham,
       Alabama and back to Boston, that triangle would con-
       tain the most important single manufacturing region
       in the world.

Exercise 26.5   Answer the following questions.

1. What is one of the keys to this country's richness?
2. What are three of the most basic needs of modern industry?
3. Does the United States contain large quantities of any of these minerals?
4. Which one is located in Pennsylvania and West Virginia?
5. Which region contains large iron-ore deposits?
6. What basic mineral do the Texas-Oklahoma and California regions contain?
7. Where is the most important single manufacturing region in the world?

≡ B.5   Observe POPULATION, SPREAD, CONCENTRATE.

Situation: Ali is talking with Mrs. Smith.

Ali: Mrs. Smith, do you know what the principal cities in the United States are?

Mrs. Smith: Yes. According to POPULATION they are New York, Chicago, Los Angeles, Philadelphia, Detroit, and Baltimore.

Ali: Is the population evenly SPREAD over the country or CONCENTRATED in one or two areas?

Mrs. Smith: It's concentrated in the East and in California.

Ali: How large is the state of Washington, D. C.?

Mrs. Smith: Washington, D. C. isn't a state, it's a city; D. C. stands for District of Columbia. As for population, it is one of our ten largest cities.

Exercise 26.6   Answer the following questions.

1. What are some of the principal cities in the United States?
2. Where is the population largely concentrated?
3. Is Washington, D. C. a state or a city?
4. How large is Washington, D. C.?
5. Why is the population largely concentrated in the East?
6. Describe the geography of your country.

Review questions.

1. Did Ali insist on talking about his impressions of the United States?
2. What did Ali enjoy owning?
3. What did John begin to tell Ali about?
4. Why isn't it easy to talk about the climate of the United States?
5. What did Ali want to know about time zones?
6. What did Nancy begin telling Ali about?
7. What did John say the basic needs of modern industry are?
8. Is it strange that principal cities, manufacturing centers, and mineral resources are located in the same region?

Lesson XXVII

A. Verbs with OUT.
B. People.
C. -ER, -ITE, -IAN: DetroitER, BrooklynITE, KentuckIAN.

≡ A.   Observe verbs with OUT.

Situation: John and his younger brother Billy are talking.

Billy: Something very strange happened to me the other day at
my club meeting. The club members had just
appointed me treasurer when a man entered our club
house. He was very excited.

John: What was he excited about?
Billy: It took us a long time to FIND that OUT. First of all,
he made us COME OUT of the club house. Then he
HANDED OUT some forms to everyone and told us
to FILL them OUT. Next we saw a man across the
street GET OUT of his car and come toward us. He
was dressed in a white uniform.

John: What did the first man look like?
Billy: Oh, I LEFT that OUT; he looked like a big Texan. Any-
way, he kept looking at the man who had gotten out of
the car. Then he seemed to recognize him and he
SHOUTED OUT, "LOOK OUT for that car," but there
wasn't any car there.

John: What happened then?
Billy: A fight BROKE OUT between the two men. After a long
time the man in the white coat won.

John: Did you find out what it was all about?
Billy: Yes, we did. After the fight, the man in the white
coat POINTED OUT that it was a make-believe fight.
The Texan was supposed to be a spy and he had to
catch him. After he told us this, he PUT OUT his
cigarette and they both left.

John: Did you believe him?
Billy: I guess so, but we never did find out what the forms
were for.

Exercise 27.1   Practice FIND OUT, HAND OUT, etc.

Examples: Teacher   Student

He discovered their plans.   He found out their plans.
He gave everyone forms.   He handed out forms.

1. He left his car.
2. He forgot to tell that part of the story.
3. A battle began between the two men.
4. They left the club house.
5. The man explained something the boys hadn't understood.
6. The boys learned something they hadn't known.
7. The Texan gave the boys forms.
8. The boys were supposed to answer the questions on the forms.
9. The Texan told the man in the white coat to be careful.
10. The man in the white coat extinguished his cigarette and left.

≡ B.1   Observe COLONY, IMMIGRATE, SETTLER, REFUGEE.

Situation: Ali is talking with Mr. Smith about the people of the
United States.

Ali: When did the United States become a country?
Mr. Smith: The Declaration of Independence was signed in
1776. At the time of the American Revolution,
the country consisted of three groups of
COLONIES: New England, Middle, and Southern.

Ali: Were the people in the colonies all from the same country?
Mr. Smith: No, people IMMIGRATED to the colonies from all
parts of Europe. Most of the first SETTLERS
in New England and in the South were English,
but those in the Middle colonies were Dutch
and Swedish.

Ali: What kind of people were the immigrants?
Mr. Smith: Many different types. For example, there were
religious REFUGEES, such as the Puritans;
they settled in New England. There were also
refugees who represented an English military
class; they settled in the South.

Ali: Did the immigrants come to the United States mainly for
religious freedom?
Mr. Smith: They came for many different reasons, and religious
freedom was certainly a major one. However,
they also came for adventure, as political prisoners, and to get rich. Generally speaking, they
all wanted to begin a new life.

Exercise 27.2   Answer the following questions.

1. What did the United States consist of at the time of the American Revolution?
2. Had the settlers all immigrated from the same country?
3. What nationality were the first settlers in New England? in the South?
4. Where did the Dutch and Swedish immigrants settle?
5. What kind of people were the immigrants?
6. Did the Puritans settle in the South?
7. Where did the refugees who represented the English military class settle?
8. Did all of the immigrants come to the United States for religious freedom?
9. What were some of the other reasons that they came?
10. Generally speaking, what did they all want to do?

≡ B.2   Observe PRACTICE, PRESERVE.

Situation: It's the next day.

> Ali: Didn't you tell me yesterday that the story of America is largely one of people attempting to put their dreams into PRACTICE?
>
> Mr. Smith: Yes, I told you something like that. I also told you that the dream of the people who came to the United States was to begin a new life.
>
> Ali: That's just what I want to ask you about. How could the dreams of all the immigrants come true?
>
> Mr. Smith: They didn't. There were both successes and failures and, naturally, those who succeeded made efforts to PRESERVE their success. But, the thing to remember is something else; namely, that those who failed did not give up. They continued to work, and to work hard, so that their children would at least have a better life than they had had.

Exercise 27.3   Answer the following questions.

1. What did Mr. Smith say that the story of America was?
2. Was it possible for the dreams of all the immigrants to come true?
3. Were there only successes, or were there also failures?
4. What did those who were successful try to do?
5. Did those who failed give up?
6. Why did they continue to work hard?

≡ C.   Observe -ER, -ITE, -IAN.

Ali: What is a person from New England called?
John: He's called a New EnglandER, just as people from the
       North, South, and Midwest are called Northerners,
       Southerners, and Midwesterners.

Ali: Would you call a person from Detroit a Detroiter?
John: Yes, but a Detroiter would also be a Midwesterner and a
       Michigander.

Ali: Is a person from Brooklyn called a Brooklyner?
John: No, he's a BrooklynITE, just as people from Denver are
       Denverites, and people from Jackson are Jacksonites.

Ali: What is a person from California called?
John: He's a CalifornIAN. People from Kentucky are
       Kentuckians. A person who lives in Philadelphia is
       both a Philadelphian and a Pennsylvanian.

Exercise 27.4   Please answer the questions.

1. What is a person from New England called?
2. What can a person from Detroit be called?
3. What are people from Brooklyn called?
4. What can a person from Philadelphia be called?
5. What are people from Texas and California called?
6. What are people from the North, South, and Midwest called?
7. What are people from Denver and Jackson called?
8. What are people from Kentucky called?

Review questions.

1. Did the club appoint John treasurer?
2. Did the Texan want the forms filled out by one boy, or by all the
   boys?
3. How long did the boys watch the two men fight?
4. What had the immigrants come to the United States planning to do?
5. Did all of the settlers find what they expected in their new home?
6. Would you call a Bostonian a Midwesterner?

Lesson XXVIII

A. GET UP, DIE DOWN, GO OUT.
B. Government and Politics.

_____

≡ A. Observe GET UP, DIE DOWN, GO OUT.

Situation: John and his father are camping in the mountains. It's
late evening. They have been sitting around the
campfire and talking.

John: Should I GET UP and put some wood on the campfire? It
seems to be DYING DOWN.
Mr. Smith: Yes. We don't want it to GO OUT yet.

(John stands up, gets some wood, and puts it on the fire. Then
he sits down again.)

John: How long do you think the fire will go on burning?
Mr. Smith: It'll probably burn for a couple of hours. Be sure to
hang your coat up near your bed tonight.

Exercise 28.1   Practice GET UP, DIE DOWN, GO OUT, etc.

Examples: Teacher	Student
While they were talking, the fire . . .	While they were talking, the fire died down.
They didn't want the fire to . . .	They didn't want the fire to go out.

1. He . . . and put some wood on the fire.
2. After he put the wood on the fire, he . . .
3. The fire began to . . . so he put some wood on it.
4. His cigar . . . so he lit it again.
5. The second time he lit his cigarette, it . . . burning.
6. He . . . in a chair.
7. The phone rang, so he . . . to answer it.
8. After he finished talking on the phone, he . . .
9. All of the lights . . . during the storm.

☰ B.1   Observe FIELD, ORGANIZATION.

Situation: After Ali had been at Riverside University for a few
            months, he decided to join the International Rela-
            tions Club. At one of the meetings he was asked
            to introduce the speaker for the evening. It was
            his adviser, Professor Jones.

> I'm very happy to be able to introduce our speaker this
> evening. Professor Jones has been at Riverside University
> since 1948. He did his undergraduate work at the University of
> Wisconsin and received his M.A. and Ph.D. in history from
> Columbia University. He has published several articles and
> books in his FIELD. He is a member of several professional
> ORGANIZATIONS and was vice-president of the American
> Historical Association in 1961. Professor Jones has agreed to
> speak to us this evening about American government and politics.

Exercise 28.2   Answer the following questions.

1. What organization did Ali join?
2. Who was the speaker for the evening?
3. What did Ali say about Professor Jones?
4. What had Professor Jones studied?
5. Had he published anything in his field?
6. What kind of organizations was Professor Jones a member of?
7. What did Professor Jones agree to speak about?

☰ B.2   Observe DEMOCRATIC, REPUBLICAN, EXECUTIVE, LEGISLA-
         TURE, JUDICIARY.

Situation: Professor Jones goes to the speaker's stand.

> I'd rather not make a long speech tonight. Since you are
> interested in government and politics, I think that an informal
> discussion will be much more interesting. Whenever you want
> to ask a question, please interrupt me.
>
> You all know, I'm sure, that the government of the United
> States is based on both DEMOCRATIC and REPUBLICAN princi-
> ples. It is democratic because the people govern themselves, and
> it is republican because the people elect their representatives
> and their chief executive.
>
> The American Constitution provides for an EXECUTIVE, a
> LEGISLATURE, and a JUDICIARY, and gives them definite
> powers. For example, the legislature, or Congress, is given the
> power to make laws. The judiciary, or Supreme Court, is given
> the power to interpret laws. And the executive, or President, is
> given the power to enforce laws. Thus, each branch of govern-
> ment has a specific independence and responsibility. In addition,
> this separation of power prevents any branch of government
> from becoming more powerful than the other two.

Exercise 28.3　　Answer the following questions.

1. Did Professor Jones intend to make a formal speech?
2. What did he give the students permission to do?
3. What kind of principles is the American government based on?
4. What are the three branches of government?
5. Which branch has the power to make laws?
6. Which branch has the power to interpret laws?
7. Which branch has the power to enforce laws?
8. Why can't one branch of the government take over the other two?
9. Why is a separation of power important?

≡ B.3　　Observe STIR UP, ELECTION, CANDIDATE, ATTITUDE.

Americans are generally more interested in politics than in government; however, their interest seems to be different from that found in many other countries.

Let me explain. Americans get very STIRRED UP about politics during presidential ELECTIONS, which are held every four years. They listen to the CANDIDATES on the radio and television and read about them in newspapers and magazines. They argue with each other and often get very excited. However, as soon as the election is over, their interest dies down and they seem to forget about politics.

This ATTITUDE toward politics often surprises foreign visitors, as does the general lack of political activity at American universities. Whereas the universities in some countries are centers of political activity, those in the United States seldom are.

Exercise 28.4　　Answer the following questions.

1. Are Americans usually more interested in politics, or in government?
2. When do Americans get stirred up about politics?
3. Who do they find out about on the radio, television, and in the press?
4. When does the excitement die down?
5. What happens as soon as the election is over?
6. What are foreign visitors often surprised at in the United States?
7. Do you find American students less interested in politics than you are?
8. What do American students seem to devote their attention to?

☰ B.4   Observe SYMBOLIZE, CONSERVATIVE, LIBERAL, TRADITION.

Situation: Several students raise their hands. Professor Jones
calls on one of them.

Koji: How many political parties are there in the United States?
Prof. Jones: We have a two-party system; that is, there are two
major parties: the Republican, SYMBOLIZED
by an elephant, and the Democratic, symbolized
by a donkey. But there are also smaller parties;
for example, the Socialist, American Labor,
and Prohibition parties.

Pedro: Are all the CONSERVATIVES in one party and all the
LIBERALS in the other?
Prof. Jones: No, there are conservatives and liberals in both
parties, and for this reason it is difficult to
make generalizations about either Republicans
or Democrats. Moreover, even though people
tend to vote according to TRADITION in some
elections, in others they vote according to the
candidates or the issues.

Exercise 28.5   Answer the following questions.

1. What are the two major political parties in the United States?
2. What symbolizes the Republican Party?
3. What symbolizes the Democratic Party?
4. What are some of the other political parties?
5. Are the conservatives in the Republican party, or in the
   Democratic party?
6. Why is it difficult to make generalizations about Republicans or
   Democrats?
7. How do some people vote?
8. Do you think a person should vote according to tradition, according to who the candidates are or according to what the issues
   are?
9. Should a person always vote for his party's candidates?

☰ B.5   Observe PRIMARY, CAMPAIGN, POLLS, MAJORITY, DELEGATE.

Harold: How does a president get elected?
Prof. Jones: There are several steps: PRIMARY elections, the
national convention, the CAMPAIGN, and the
POLLS. First, the person must prove that the
voters prefer him to others in his party by win-
ning some primary elections. Then, he must get
a MAJORITY of the DELEGATES at his party's
national convention to select him as their candidate. Next, he must campaign around the country
for votes. And finally, he must win the support of
a majority of the people at the polls in November.

Exercise 28.6   Answer the following questions.

1. How does a person become president of the United States?
2. What must he prove in a primary election?
3. What must he do at his party's national convention?
4. What must each candidate do before election day?
5. What must he win at the polls?
6. Who decides which person will be the president?

Review questions.

1. Having gotten some wood and put it on the fire, what did John do?
2. Is sitting around a campfire enjoyable?
3. Having been at the university for a few months, what did Ali do?
4. Did Professor Jones think that speaking informally would be much less interesting?
5. Why does listening to presidential candidates stir people up?
6. Did Professor Jones say that generalizing about a Republican or a Democrat was easy?
7. Having won a primary election, what is a presidential candidate's next step?
8. Is campaigning for votes very important in an election?

Lesson XXIX

A. DROP BY, GIVE UP.
B. GET AWAY WITH, STAY AWAY FROM, LOOK OUT FOR.
C. UNkind, DISagree, MISunderstand, INformal, IMproper.

☰ A. Observe DROP BY, GIVE UP.

Situation: When Mrs. Smith woke up this morning, she had a
very bad pain in her side.

> Mrs. Smith: Dear, please call up Dr. Brown and find out if
> he can DROP BY for a few minutes.
>
> Mr. Smith: (He phones Dr. Brown.) Nobody answers.
> Mrs. Smith: Please keep trying. My side is getting worse.
>
> Mr. Smith: Don't worry. I won't GIVE UP until I can get him.

NOTE: DROP BY means *visit*.

Exercise 29.1   Practice DROP BY, GIVE UP, etc.

Examples: Teacher	Student
Mr. Smith phoned the doctor. He wanted him to come to the house.	Mr. Smith called up the doctor. He wanted him to drop by the house.

1. His wife said, "Please keep trying."
2. He didn't stop trying.
3. The doctor visited her for a few minutes.
4. He discovered what the pain was.
5. They invited him to visit them sometime.
6. I went to see you yesterday, but nobody was home.
7. He almost lost all hope of learning English.
8. He couldn't guess the answer, so he stopped trying.
9. Come and see us whenever you can.

≡ B.   Observe GET AWAY WITH, STAY AWAY FROM, LOOK OUT FOR.

> Mrs. Smith: This afternoon I got through with my housework
>   earlier than I expected to, so I decided to pick
>   up some groceries. I drove to the shopping
>   center, got out of the car, and began walking
>   toward the grocery store. Then I noticed a
>   large number of policemen.
>
> Mr. Smith: What were they doing?
>
> Mrs. Smith: They seemed to be looking for someone. I didn't
>   pay much attention to them. Later one of the
>   clerks told me that someone had stolen an
>   expensive camera.
>
> Mr. Smith: Did he GET AWAY WITH it?
>
> Mrs. Smith: No, they caught him. Although he successfully
>   STAYED AWAY FROM the policemen, he
>   forgot to LOOK OUT FOR the store detectives.

Exercise 29.2   Practice GET AWAY WITH, STAY AWAY FROM,
                 LOOK OUT FOR.

Examples: <u>Teacher</u>   <u>Student</u>

Mrs. Smith finished her housework.   Mrs. Smith got through with her
                                       housework.

She opened the car door and got out.   She got out of the car.

1. Someone tried to steal an expensive camera.
2. He didn't go near the police.
3. However, he forgot to watch for the store detectives.
4. Another person tried to steal a car.
5. Her mother told her not to go near the water.
6. Children must learn to be careful of cars.
7. The man said, "Watch out!"

≡ C.1   Observe UN-.

Situation: John is having dinner with Pedro.

> Pedro: Did you get to class on time this morning?
> John: No, UNFORTUNATELY I overslept again. How was your
>   class?
>
> Pedro: It was so UNINTERESTING that I fell asleep.
> John: Did the teacher ask you any questions?
>
> Pedro: Yes. I was UNPLEASANTLY awakened by a very
>   UNUSUAL question.
> John: That was very UNKIND of your teacher. Were you able to
>   answer it?
> Pedro: No, I was UNABLE to.

Exercise 29.3   Practice UN-.

Examples: <u>Teacher</u>   <u>Student</u>

Was the class lecture interesting?   No, it was uninteresting.
Was it necessary to bring an um-   No, it was unnecessary to
  brella today?   bring an umbrella today.
Do you lock the door before you   No, you unlock the door before
  enter a building?   you enter a building.

1. Was it fortunate that John overslept?
2. Did the professor give an interesting lecture this morning?
3. Was John pleasantly awakened?
4. Did the professor ask him a usual question?
5. Was he able to answer the question?
6. Did he give a satisfactory answer?
7. Did John think the teacher was kind?
8. Is the chair you're sitting on comfortable?
9. Do you button your coat before you take it off?
10. Is it pleasant to take examinations?

≡ C.2   Observe DIS-.

Situation: Nancy is talking with her mother.

Nancy: Did you ever meet anyone as DISAGREEABLE as Jim?
Mrs. Smith: I don't think he's disagreeable. On the contrary,
            I find him very agreeable.

Nancy: I DISLIKE HIM very much. He always DISAGREES
        with what I say.
Mrs. Smith: Oh, I see!

Exercise 29.4   Practice DIS-.

Examples: <u>Teacher</u>   <u>Student</u>

Jim isn't very agreeable.   Jim is very disagreeable
Nancy says she doesn't like him.   Nancy says she dislikes him.

1. He never agrees with anything she says.
2. He is never pleased with what she says.
3. She is rarely honest when she gives her age.
4. She doesn't like any kind of candy.
5. They decided not to continue the course.
6. She wasn't pleased with their homework.
7. He didn't do his work honestly.
8. She said she didn't like football.

☰ C.3   Observe MIS-.

Situation: Ali and Nancy are watching television.

> Nancy: Did you have a test today?
> Ali: Yes, it was my MISFORTUNE to have one in pronunciation.
> Nancy: Had you studied for it?
> Ali: No, I hadn't. First I MISUNDERSTOOD the directions,
>   then I MISPRONOUNCED some of the sentences, and
>   finally I MISSPELLED several words.

Exercise 29.5   Practice MIS-.

Examples: <u>Teacher</u>   <u>Student</u>

Ali didn't understand the directions.   Ali misunderstood the directions.
He spelled the words wrong.   He mispelled the words.

1. He didn't pronounce his sentence correctly.
2. He didn't spell the words right.
3. He didn't understand what the teacher said.
4. He was so sleepy that he spelled his name wrong.
5. Although he studied hard, he still pronounced some words wrong.
6. He didn't understand because he was sleepy.
7. Although he practiced the word, he still spelled it wrong.
8. He pronounced the word incorrectly because he had forgotten
    the rule.
9. Their leader led them in the wrong direction.

☰ C.4   Observe IN-, IM-.

Situation: Pedro and Nancy are at a picnic the day after
            Professor Jones's talk on politics.

> Pedro: What a nice looking outfit! You look like a million
>   dollars.
> Nancy: Do you like it? It was very INEXPENSIVE.
> Pedro: IMPOSSIBLE! I'm sure it must've cost a great deal.
>
> Nancy: How was your meeting last night?
> Pedro: Very informative. Professor Jones gave an INFORMAL
>   talk and allowed us to interrupt him whenever we
>   wanted to.
>
> Nancy: Isn't it IMPROPER to interrupt someone when he's
>   giving a speech?
> Pedro: No, not when he's speaking INFORMALLY.

Exercise 29.6   Practice IN-, IM-.

Examples: Teacher   Student

Her new outfit wasn't expensive.   Her new outfit was inexpensive.
Professor Jones didn't give a   Professor Jones gave an informal
   formal talk.   talk.

1. She thought that it wasn't proper to interrupt a speaker.
2. It wasn't possible for him to take a vacation.
3. He said, "Since it's not a formal dance, you can wear anything."
4. It isn't polite to make noise when you eat soup or drink tea.
5. He didn't answer the question correctly.
6. They thought that it wasn't possible to fly to the moon.
7. His new suit didn't cost very much.
8. He thought that it wouldn't be possible for him to learn English.

Review questions.

1. Did Mr. Smith call up Dr. Brown as a result of his wife's pain,
    or in spite of his wife's pain?
2. Since the man who stole the camera stayed away from the police-
    men, did he, therefore, get away?
3. What happened to Pedro as a consequence of his uninteresting
    class?
4. Nancy thought Jim was disagreeable, but, on the other hand,
    what did Mrs. Smith think?
5. Even though Nancy says that she finds Jim disagreeable, does she,
    in fact, dislike him?
6. What did Ali do in addition to misunderstanding the test directions?
7. Professor Jones spoke informally. Consequently, was it proper or
    improper to interrupt him?

Lesson XXX

A. Review.

Exercise 30.1

Examples: Teacher	Student
The young lady was <u>trying to find</u> something.	The young lady was looking for something.
Professors usually <u>ask</u> students <u>questions</u>.	Professors usually call on students.

1. Mary wanted to <u>request</u> something but forgot.
2. Larry asked if he could <u>pick</u> her <u>up</u> at seven.
3. Jim <u>visited</u> all of his relatives before he left.
4. Pedro woke up when the teacher <u>asked</u> him <u>a question</u>.
5. Henry learned that he <u>didn't need</u> a dictionary.
6. Bob got up, <u>saw</u> the snow, and went back to bed.
7. Jack is <u>trying to find</u> his homework assignment.
8. Robert can seldom <u>remember</u> the right answer.
9. Susan said, "Please <u>don't go without</u> me."
10. <u>Serving</u> customers kept the clerk busy.
11. Jean's father <u>takes</u> two daily newspapers.
12. Mr. Smith <u>met</u> an old friend in town.

Exercise 30.2

Examples: Teacher	Student
You may <u>omit</u> question 13.	You may leave out question 13.
Please <u>put</u> everything <u>under your chair</u>.	Please put everything away.

1. Margaret said that she <u>was raised</u> in Arizona.
2. James wanted to <u>ask</u> something.
3. They had to <u>cancel</u> the picnic because of the weather.
4. He gave them a form and asked them to <u>answer the questions</u>.
5. The professor <u>returned</u> the term papers.
6. They <u>gave</u> their assignments to the teacher.
7. The examinations were <u>distributed</u>.
8. The bride <u>wore</u> a white dress.
9. The teacher told them to <u>omit</u> the third question.
10. You can <u>find</u> addresses in the telephone book.
11. Tom <u>packed</u> his winter clothes <u>away</u>.

Exercise 30.3

Examples: Teacher	Student
The firemen extinguished the fire.	The firemen put out the fire.
People often get excited about politics.	People often get stirred up about politics.

1. Mr. Jones decided to postpone the test.
2. Many students had worn non-western clothes.
3. The students extinguished their cigarettes.
4. The lady bent down to get her groceries.
5. The teacher said, "Next week we'll discuss dating."
6. Robert put on several suits before he bought one.
7. He called attention to the main problem.
8. He borrowed three library books.
9. He got so excited that he started a fight.

Exercise 30.4

Examples: Teacher	Student
What did you do after you . . . your homework?	What did you do after you got through with your homework?
When the fire . . ., he put some wood on it.	When the fire died down, he put some wood on it.

1. I'll call you up as soon as I . . . my assignment.
2. Donald . . . at seven every morning.
3. He . . . talking so long that I went to sleep.
4. The lights . . . all over the city.
5. Always remember to . . . the phone.
6. He usually . . . in his favorite chair.
7. When she came in, all the men . . .
8. The excitement . . . after each election.
9. Ali . . . and introduced the speaker.

Exercise 30.5

Examples: Teacher	Student
His friends came to see him.	His friends dropped by to see him.
Bad weather delayed the plane.	Bad weather held up the plane.

1. Jane wanted him to phone her.
2. They finally discovered what the problem was.
3. They didn't stop trying to learn.
4. Jim stopped sleeping when the phone rang.
5. An accident delayed the bus for an hour.
6. He said, "I came to see how you are."
7. He phoned the doctor and made an appointment.
8. She wanted to know what had delayed him.
9. They tried to discover who the man was.
10. Their friend stopped trying to learn Spanish.

Exercise 30.6

Examples: <u>Teacher</u>   <u>Student</u>

The thief <u>escaped with</u> $10,000.   The thief got away with $10,000.
He <u>didn't go to bed</u> until midnight.   He stayed up until midnight.

1. Mr. and Mrs. Smith <u>seldom quarreled.</u>
2. The man almost <u>stole</u> a camera.
3. There are many things you should <u>be careful of.</u>
4. She never goes to the store until she <u>uses</u> everything <u>up.</u>
5. He <u>seldom goes to bed</u> until one o'clock in the morning.
6. Three of the prisoners <u>escaped.</u>
7. She got frightened when he said, "<u>Be careful!</u>"
8. He <u>spent his last dollar</u> three days ago.

Exercise 30.7   Review verbs with UP.

a. *Completion.*

Examples: <u>Teacher</u>   <u>Student</u>

What did Harry do with his food?   He ate it up.
What did Jerry do with his watch?   He wound it up.

1. What did Sue do with her dirty room?
2. What did Dave do with his money?
3. What did Ann do with the unfinished letter?
4. What did Sue do with her clean room?
5. What did Carol do with the empty glass?
6. What did Donald do with his milk?

b. *Elevation.*

Examples: <u>Teacher</u>   <u>Student</u>

Mrs. Smith dropped some groceries.   Then she picked them up.
Bob sat down for a while.   Then he stood up.

1. Eddie carried the flag over to the flagpole.
2. Lynn's mother told her to get out of bed.
3. Ann finished talking on the telephone.
4. Mr. Hansen dropped his keys on the ground.
5. Sally sat down to eat breakfast.
6. Jack's alarm clock rang.
7. Carol took her coat off near the coat rack.

Exercise 30.8   Review verbs with OVER.

a. *Again.*

Examples: <u>Teacher</u>   <u>Student</u>

The teacher said, "Please do   The teacher said, "Please do
   this exercise again."   this exercise over."
He had to write the composition   He had to write the composi-
   again.   tion over.

1. They asked him to play the record again.
2. They made her sing the song a second time.
3. He corrected the letter and she typed it again.
4. They asked him to retell the story.
5. The little boy had to wash his hands again.
6. They rewrote the poem.
7. The story-teller retold his story.

b. *Examine*.

Examples: <u>Teacher</u>   <u>Student</u>

Gary examined the car visually.   He looked the car over.
Rosa examined the composition   She went over the composition.
  generally.

1. Bill examined the plans mentally.
2. Joyce and Helen discussed their plans.
3. Dick examined the room visually.
4. Mary examined the two possibilities mentally.
5. Charles examined the application generally.
6. David and Bill discussed the problem.

Exercise 30.9   Review verbs with BACK: *return*.

Examples: <u>Teacher</u>   <u>Student</u>

He arrived early in the morning.   He got back early in the
                                       morning.

He returned to school after the   He went back to school after
  vacation.   the vacation.

1. Bill intends to return to his country next month.
2. He'll probably go by plane.
3. However, he'd like to go by car.
4. One of his friends asked, ''Why don't you go by foot?''
5. He arrived one month later.
6. The teacher returned the students' papers.
7. John returned the library book by mail.
8. He took her book, looked it over, and returned it.
9. Students always like to return here.
10. Dave returned the book to the library.

Exercise 30.10   Review verbs with ON: *continue*.

Examples: <u>Teacher</u>   <u>Student</u>

Sue didn't wake up until ten.   Sue slept on until ten.
Bill left Detroit and went to   Bill left Detroit and flew on
  Miami by plane.   to Miami.

1. The alarm clock <u>continued</u> ringing.
2. He tried to <u>continue sleeping</u> until noon.
3. He <u>continued driving</u> for three hours.
4. He wanted to <u>continue</u> but he was too sleepy.
5. He left Denver and <u>went</u> to Seattle <u>by plane.</u>
6. He left Seattle and <u>went</u> to Hawaii <u>by ship.</u>
7. The bell <u>wouldn't stop</u> ringing.
8. He <u>didn't wake up</u> until one in the afternoon.
9. He <u>couldn't stop</u> thinking about the story for a week.
10. He tried <u>not to stop.</u>

Exercise 30.11   Review verbs with ABOUT: *regarding.*

Examples: <u>Teacher</u>   <u>Student</u>

Did Tom talk last night?   Yes, he talked about dating.
  . . . dating
Did Joan sing last Friday?   Yes, she sang about life in her
  . . . life in her country.   country.

1. Are you thinking? . . . the examination tomorrow
2. Is Mr. A worried? . . . the two-word verbs
3. Did Mr. B smile? . . . what you said
4. Did you dream last night? . . . my family
5. Are you wondering, Mr. E? . . . the meaning of dreams
6. Do you dream, Mr. F? . . . speaking English
7. Why is everyone smiling? . . . speaking English in dreams
8. Are you worried, Mr. H? . . . forgetting my native language
9. What are you wondering, Mr. I? . . . the examination tomorrow
10. What are you thinking, Mr. J? . . . the end of the course

ANSWERS

NOTE: The answers are given in their dictionary form; the tense and
  word order may have to be adjusted to fit the context.

Exercise 30.1   Exercise 30.2   Exercise 30.3

1. ask for   1. bring up   1. put off
2. call for   2. bring up   2. put on
3. call on   3. call off   3. put out
4. call on   4. fill out   4. pick up
5. can do without   5. give back   5. take up
6. look at   6. hand in   6. try on
7. look for   7. hand out   7. point out
8. think of   8. have on   8. check out
9. wait for   9. leave out   9. stir up
10. wait on   10. look up
11. subscribe to   11. put away
12. run into

Exercise 30.4

1. get through with
2. get up
3. go on
4. go out
5. hang up
6. sit down
7. stand up
8. die down
9. get up

Exercise 30.5

1. call up
2. find out
3. give up
4. wake up
5. hold up
6. drop by
7. call up
8. hold up
9. find out
10. give up

Exercise 30.6

1. get along
2. get away with
3. look out for
4. run out of
5. stay up
6. get away
7. look out
8. run out of

Exercise 30.7a

1. clean up
2. use up
3. finish up
4. dirty up
5. fill up
6. drink up

Exercise 30.7b

1. put up
2. get up
3. hang up
4. pick up
5. stand up, get up
6. get up
7. hang up

Exercise 30.8a

1. play over
2. sing over
3. type over
4. tell over
5. wash over
6. write over
7. tell over

Exercise 30.8b

1. think over
2. talk over
3. look over
4. think over
5. go over
6. talk over

Exercise 30.9

1. go back
2. fly back
3. drive back
4. walk back
5. get back
6. give back
7. send back
8. give back
9. come back
10. take back

Exercise 30.10

1. keep on, go on
2. sleep on
3. drive on
4. go on, keep on
5. fly on
6. sail on
7. keep on, go on
8. sleep on
9. keep on, go on
10. go on, keep on

Exercise 30.11

1. think about
2. worry about
3. smile about
4. dream about
5. wonder about
6. dream about
7. smile about
8. worry about
9. wonder about
10. think about